ENCOUNTERS WITH LEADERSHIP

[14] Do not neglect your gift, which you were given through a prophecy when the body of elders gave you s'mikhah. [15] Be diligent about this work, throw yourself into it, so that your progress may be clear to everyone. [16] Pay attention to yourself and to the teaching, continue in it, for by so doing you will deliver both yourself and those who hear you. Complete Jewish Bible

By John W. & Pamela K. Dillon—Pastors

Author Prophetess Pamela K. Dillon

To _____

Date: _____

ENCOUNTERS with LEADERSHIP—

PRODUCING AND PROMOTING HEALTHY LEADERS

*Handbook and Manual of Mentorship
and Fellowship*

PAMELA K. DILLON

WestBow
PRESS
A DIVISION OF THOMAS NELSON

WestBow Press books may be ordered through booksellers or by contacting:

WestBow Press
A Division of Thomas Nelson
1663 Liberty Drive
Bloomington, IN 47403
www.westbowpress.com
1 (866) 928-1240

ISBN: 978-1-4908-1220-5 (sc)

Library of Congress Control Number: 2013918631

Printed in the United States of America.

WestBow Press rev. date: 10/18/2013

John and Pamela Dillon clearly understand their role in the Kingdom of God; to usher in the presence of God and to produce and promote God's leaders for service to His people, the Body of Christ, through mentorship and fellowship. John and Pamela complement each other with undeniable unity and sequence of spirit.

John & Pamela Dillon are the founders and pastors of the innovative *Agape Time Ministries—City of Refuge in St. Louis, Missouri.* Together they have over 25 years of ministry experience. While they are uniquely different in personality, together they bring skill, experience, and knowledge to the heart of each believer equipping those who partake of their ministry to walk out their God given assignments. Those who encounter their ministry whether, individually or as a team, find them to be interpersonal, engaging, approachable, and dynamic in presentation.

In addition to carrying out her duties as a pastor and mentor, Pamela is the published author of *The Greater Yes—Answering the Call of God"(2009), Give Him the Ashes" (2004), "Thank God for Pookie'nem?-a look a Christian relationships" (1999). They are hosts and founders of the "Stir Up the Gift Summit" (1997) and "The Intimate Evening with the Father" (2005), and Expression Sunday.*

John and Pamela believe that one of their greatest accomplishments are the Leaders of Agape Time who have set their hearts to seek a relationship with God the Father and lock into the responsibility of being developed for healthy Kingdom living as they walk out their vocations and elections.

John and Pamela are the happy parents of 4 adult children, 8 grandchildren, 1 great grandchild, and a host of spiritual sons & daughters. For booking and more information, contact them at: Agape Time Ministries, Inc.-City of Refuge

2280 North Waterford Drive, Florissant, MO 63033, 314-830-1784, mailing address: P.O. Box 755, Florissant, Mo 63032, www.facebook.com/Agape Time Ministries—City of Refuge

Email: atmi2000@sbcglobal.net.

OTHER BOOKS AND MANUALS BY PAMELA K. DILLON

"Thank God For Pookie'nem"—1999
"Give Him The Ashes"—2004
"The Greater Yes—Answering The Call of God"—2009
"Stir Up the Prophetic In You"

TABLE OF CONTENTS

INTRODUCTION

INTRODUCTION

What we have come to know.

We have come to know that people really do want to know their identity in the body of Christ. People of God really want to experience the true fellowship of the Holy Spirit. In addition, they want to experience this same love and fellowship through God's people—in particular His leadership—on a more intimate level.

This requirement of intimacy and personal fellowship is not a new concept. Jesus the Christ pioneered this vision over 2000 years ago. Jesus ate, slept, had fun, ministered alongside and taught the disciples on an intimate level. The disciples, known as the 12 apostles, continued this style of fellowship throughout the establishment of the early church as found in Acts 2:42

The Fellowship of the Believers

[42] They devoted themselves to the apostles' teaching and to fellowship, to the breaking of bread and to prayer. [43] Everyone was filled with awe at the many wonders and signs performed by the apostles. [44] All the believers were together and had everything in common. [45] They sold property and possessions to give to anyone who had need. [46] Every day they continued to meet together in the temple courts. They broke bread in their homes and ate together with glad and sincere hearts, [47] praising God and enjoying the favor of all the people. And the Lord added to their number daily those who were being saved.

We understand that this is a costly endeavor and that everyone may not be called to this type of one on one relationship with those they endeavor to disciple. However, this type of relationship is critical to bring those leaders around you to a different standard in their callings. *John Maxwell* put it so beautifully in his book *The 21 Irrefutable Laws of Leadership . . . "You must develop 20 who will pour into the 80."*

Today more than ever, the world is calling out to the body of Christ to listen to them, talk to them, and assist them in being delivered and walking in freedom. Moreover, Christians are asking Leadership to mentor them, help establish, and spend quality time in a one on one or small group setting. The primary reason is that many desire to develop a relationship with God. People are basically asking for discipleship. Mentorship is the politically correct way to express this need in this generation.

Through direct experience we have come to know that to have powerfully equipped and healthy leaders you must develop them in a setting that allows them to be taught, be provided feedback, express their gifting, be accountable and, most of all, be in a tangible relationship they can trust.

In this handbook, we endeavor to give some practical tools that we have used in developing leaders with great success. Of course we do not claim to have the monopoly on this business. There are many other great and far more experience people who have written and taught on this subject. Our desire is to add our portion to what God is requiring at this moment.

Several times we were encouraged by some prolific leaders around the country to write a book and design a manual that would give the tools we have used to develop those in our ministry. It was very evident that something different was going on in our ministry because of the excessive spiritual growth in the leaders we pastor.

One thing in particular that stands out is the age genre attracted to the ministry. Young adults between 17 years old to 30 years old find the Agape Time to be relevant, relational, and refreshing. Mature adults find it to be a place of refuge and restoration. The two generations connect to cause an explosion of energy, wisdom, and power for change. In the past, generations have been divided to be taught and to grow spiritually. There is some utility to that method, but it has been taken to a far extreme.

One of our young adult leaders said to me one day, "I have been looking around for the older people that would teach the younger like the scripture says, <u>Titus 2:3</u> (**NKJV**) the **older** women likewise, that they be reverent in behavior, not slanderers, not given to much wine, **teach**ers of good things—"but no one really wanted to be bothered."

The sting in her words was truth. The mature in age generation have a different set of issues but like concerns. Those concerns are primarily abuse in ministry, lack of training, and lack of character. We found that there is a power in having the generations walk alongside mentoring one another. One generation has wisdom gained through experience, trial and error, while the other offers fresh zeal, intense warfare, and a willingness to pursue God. The fusion of wisdom with zeal shall perform the work in the last days to come.

In order to meet the needs of Christians coming to the church for fellowship, we have to change what it church looks like. We, of course, are not suggesting changing the message of Christ. However, we must expand its borders. In this way, we surround ourselves with resources to develop our congregates. We must make the Christian experience an interactive commitment and give those who desire to grow in relationship and leadership in God a more hands on experience. A place where they can be birthed out and/or established in their God-given talents, gifts, and callings. Some are calling these houses, Apostolic Centers. It is viable part of the church, not a separate entity.

In the past 10 years we have seen the rise of house churches. Again, people of God want a more intimate setting. House churches offer a genuine sense of family, accountability, freedom in the spirit, and intimacy in a small group setting of learning the word and interacting. However there is an additional process that must take place. One must be able to not only learn the word of God through teaching, one must be able to have intense training, development, and equipping in several leadership roles.

We must set an atmosphere of fellowship that promotes spiritual growth on an individual basis. In doing so we must question the church-goers, the born again believer, and ask, "Do you know who you are? Furthermore would you like to develop who you are for the cause of Christ?" This had not been accomplished by our present day style, of being seated in pews only, week after week applauding for the stage presentation that has grown spectacular in its presentation. Nor has it been achieved by lobbying and posturing to be a part of a specific auxiliaries, or ministries within the church.

What we have come to know is that marketplace anointing and the church anointing must combine to advance the kingdom of God. We have come to know that team ministry in every presentation, husband and wife, or trained leaders leaving their camp or church to work side by side to prophesy, pray, and minister as a team, congruently on the same platform.

What we have come to know is that the church in its present form has no legs. We have spiritual ears to hear, prophetic voices to proclaim, anointed eyes to see visions and purpose and yet on a whole we are not walking. We are not really moving forward as a family, and as sons of God. Why? Because we are missing a limb. The ability to walk requires a body, not only as an isolated part or a group of parts.

Apostolic Centers or Leadership Development houses are the legs we need to walk. It is not a separate entity but an extension of the church. It could be seen as participating in an on the job training program or a practicum and then obtaining your true job.

In the following pages you will find tools to assist you in producing and promoting healthy leaders in your church, or business. You will find sample forms and topics to discuss, as well testimonials and pictures from our ministry exploits. We would love your feedback. Please find our contact information at the back of the manual.

STIR UP THE GIFT

2 Timothy 1:6 New King James Version (NKJV)[6] Therefore I remind you to stir up the gift of God which is in you through the laying on of my hands.

2 Timothy 1:6 New International Version (NIV) Appeal for Loyalty to Paul and the Gospel [6] For this reason I remind you to fan into flame the gift of God, which is in you through the laying on of my hands.

Our Agape Time logo has a thunderous message, proclaiming the ministry and vision of Agape Time. It speaks intently. At first glance, the cauldron with the flames of fire emerging from the pot and the heart which is situated in the midst of the flames captivates your interest. One will sense in looking upon it that something is happening here is very powerful. The heart of God is producing something active and alive.

The history of the logo is both prophetic and comical. In my zeal to please the Lord at the inception of the ministry in 1997, I designed a logo which was not at all original. It was the symbol of the baby cupid with a bow and arrow targeted at a heart. After all, the ministry was conceived through the Holy Spirit on the morning of February 14, 1995. Consequently, the cupid—at the time anyway—seemed to be the ideal logo for Agape Time Ministries. But this borrowed baby cupid logo was far from what the spirit of the Lord had birthed Agape Time to do in the earth.

My dear friend, Marsha Walters, happened to be talking with me about the new ministry God had given me and asked to see the pamphlet I had created. To my surprise she began laughing hysterically. The baby cupid tickled her. She said, "Pam, Pam. This baby does not at all reflect the work of the ministry of Agape Time." Of course I was just a little tart annoyed by her response but I agreed to allow her to pray and to design a more appropriate logo for the ministry.

Marsha did have a gift in administration and design. She had the wisdom of God to present ministries or business to the public on paper with a powerful reflection of the heart of God in a single picture. This creativity manifested as a cauldron with a heart surrounded by flames and white strip going across the heart. When I saw it, I was in awe of the impartation it made in my heart. The logo spoke very descriptively about the vision of Agape Time and its work in the earth. Thus the logo for Agape Time was born.

Years later in 2002, Pastor John added yet another powerful statement to the logo. The cauldron was sitting flat and he elevated the cauldron by placing it on top of a column and raising the standard.

So what does all this symbolism mean? At a glance the logo speaks of the mission we have towards God's people to Stir up the Gift of God in them. The flames represent the work of the Holy Spirit in an individual's life. The work of the Holy Spirit sets the gift aflame. The fire is twofold in its administration. The Holy Spirit's consuming fire burns out what you don't need. It refines your gift for an increasing anointing in the process. The cauldron represents the altar in that you must present yourself as a living sacrifice. The cauldron speaks of the process of dying to oneself and giving one's life over to God. The cauldron represents getting rid of the hurt and healing and disposing of the ashes of life.

After the process is completed on many levels, one will receive a pure heart. The pure heart represents the white ribbon across the heart. After completing the process through the Holy Spirit of dying to one's life and being resurrected to his or her God-ordained life, the Leader is ready to be a servant of the Most High God.

When leaders come to the ministry, one of the most important questions asked is "are you filled with the gift of the Holy Spirit.?" Whether the answer is "yes" or "no" we start the work. We know that the assignment on the Leaders lives cannot be perfected until he or she receives the ultimate gift. This is the gift of the Holy Ghost. We spare nothing in being aggressive about the baptism of the Holy Ghost. With Godly wisdom we pursue the soul of the leader with love. When the evidence of the Holy Spirit is witnessed and confirmed by God, what applause goes on in heaven and by the surrounding team mates! We now have cooperation to do the work. The spirit of truth has entered the temple—the temple of the believer. Now the process of being developed is attainable. We want the aspiring leader to understand that there are two types of leaders on the battlefield. One of the leaders is fighting for self and the other leader is a servant of God. One leader operates as demonstrated in II Timothy delivering the message to the itching ears having great gatherings and many followers. Then there is the servant of God who wants transformation of God's people. The servant leader teaches repentance, holiness, and relationship with God.

For the time will come when people will not put up with sound doctrine. Instead, to suit their own desires, they will gather around them a great number of teachers to say what their **itching ears** want to hear. 2 Timothy 4:3

Contrary to popular belief, there are many very gifted leaders who work in the kingdom of God yet have never been filled with the Holy Spirit. as the Word tells us in Matthew

24:24, For false messiahs and false prophets will appear and perform great signs and wonders to deceive, **if possible,** even **the elect.**

Our job in producing healthy leaders is that they not be false messiahs, messengers or false prophets and they know when they have encountered a counterfeit. The process of dying to self and not being entangled with performance and greed is a must for pure motive. The spiritual and emotional health of the leader determines his or her longevity. One must be filled with the Holy Ghost and be led by this same Holy Ghost. In the last days, the Holy Ghost in operation through the sons of God will make the difference.

"'In the last days, **God** says, I will pour out my Spirit on all people. Your **sons** and daughters will prophesy, your young men will see visions, your old men will dream dreams. Acts 2:17

Identity is the key to fulfillment in life and purpose. Knowing who you are comes with knowing your Creator. Stir up the Gift means, to me, to stir up my identity. Stir up the ultimate gift the Holy Ghost, who knows all things. When you find your identity you find your purpose. Once you find your purpose, there is no way you can continue as a robot or a clone, acting and doing what others are doing without a mind or vision of your own. Your eternal identity sets you apart to complete a mission.

In the natural, our identity comes from our parents being intimate one with another. This, of course, is how a child is conceived. This child is carried in the incubator of it mother's well of living waters or spiritual womb. At any time during the pregnancy when the mother speaks, the baby identifies with the voice and has a reaction. The reaction may be a hiccup, kick, or a elbow. When the child is born there is a reaction to their parents' voice and the manifestation of the response to the mother's or father's voice is seen by everyone. On lookers will say the baby knows the voice of his mama or daddy by the way he laughs, coos, or becomes startled.

In the spirit, the connection is almost the same but to an enhanced degree. After all, now it is our Heavenly Father, who formed us in our mother's womb. His voice called us into existence and placed each of us in an earthly body. After the initial earthly birth, we are born again and received the baptism of the Holy Spirit. There is an awakening to a voice that we have heard before in eternity past. We must have the infilling of the Holy Spirit to recognize this voice. The voice makes a witness and confirmation that we are related. Now you have firsthand knowledge that you are a son of God.

After a while of listening to the voice of the Lord and obeying the voice, onlookers began to witness the relationship you have with the Father. It is called "the anointing." The anointing rests on you and stirs up in you simultaneously. This anointing begins to shape you, mold you, and identify your gift and purpose in the earth. You began to make your election and your calling sure by the stirring up of the gift. The gift of the Holy Ghost and also by expression.

For many are called (invited and summoned), but **few** are **chosen**. Matthew 22:14 In the same breath, it connects you with your creator God and with your fellow brethren to complete the great commission. The great commission incorporates us all.

The Great Commission Matthew 28: 16-20

[16] Then the eleven disciples went to Galilee, to the mountain where Jesus had told them to go. [17] When they saw him, they worshiped him; but some doubted. [18] Then Jesus came to them and said, "All authority in heaven and on earth has been given to me. [19] Therefore go and make disciples of all nations, baptizing them in the name of the Father and of the Son and of the Holy Spirit, [20] and teaching them to obey everything I have commanded you. And surely I am with you always, to the very end of the age."

One of the climaxes of the year is our "Stir up the Gift Summit". The summit is a gathering of remnant leaders to hear the voice of God for their next assignment and instructions. God calls out holy men and women to impart, embrace, and encourage those who are in ministry and those aspiring to be in ministry.

The Summit is in its 17th year at the writing of this manual. The Summit was the first assignment ever given by the Lord for the ministry. The Lord prophetically speaks during this week to the ministry gifts. During this week the deep calls unto the deep.

The atmosphere is charged with the DNA of the Lord Almighty. Ministries are identified, birthed, restored, and equipped for the next seasons to come. In addition, it is a week of rest, rejuvenation, and inspirational fellowship. The summit participant walks away from the Summit having been challenged and charged to complete the assignments set before them.

One of the goals of the Stir up the Gift Summit is that as individuals and a corporate body we link together to complete our God given assignments and realized that the Great Commission has been given to us all to complete as a body and as a team.

Our quest is to locate our purpose in the assignment and find ourselves knitted together alongside fellow brothers and sisters in Christ to complete the Great Commission mandate. Each tribe, village, or ministry camp, (sometimes referred to as a denomination or a church) has a specific assignment. Some feed the hungry, some train the troops, and some evangelize.

Activate or Stir Up the Gift of the Holy Spirit in you. Remember your Life is Light and Power in Motion to complete purpose.

MONDAY NIGHT PRAYER

You Must be a sacrifice before you can become an offering.

Presently our training facility is a very intimate setting. We intend to continue in this style of fellowship. On Monday nights when you enter into the sanctuary, the chairs are set in a large circle. The circle reflects the eternal and unending love of our Father God. In the center of the circle is the tabernacle furnishing being taught that week. I use a visual to teach causing a more impactful and effective learning moment. The tabernacle furnishings are handmade by my husband, John. It is amazing to behold the beauty and craftsmanship the Holy Spirit has endowed him with to complete these replicas of the Mosaic Tabernacle. You will sense a time of fellowship one with another and with the Father. John and I agree that if we had to choose one single act of service that causes people of God to grow, it would be prayer. Prayer is the vehicle into God's presence. I personally believe it is the mode of transportation that moves me from one place to another in the spirit and in the natural. Connecting with God in prayer is the ultimate intimate conversation. In prayer, God is able to reveal divine secrets that at any other time would be taken lightly, or not received at all.

It is the glory of God to conceal a matter; to **search out** a matter is the glory of kings. Proverbs 25:2

Prayer I believe is not a time of just asking the Father to fulfill our many needs. Prayer is quality time spent with the Father. It is the love language that elevates a soul. Prayer is two way dialogue that unifies in a moment of earth time to a eternal conversation that transcends all time. God can tell you something in one second that will propel you into a life time of freedom. A life time of prosperity. God in his awesome power is able to promote you in your ministry or career on your knees. People will be able to partake of this manifestation of anointing and it is undeniable that is the power of Ruach Hakodesh the Hebrew word for the Holy Spirit.

There is nothing in your ministry that can replace prayer. You can read all the books on any given subject, and even read the Holy Bible. You can even fast but if you don't pray, your fasting is to no avail. Until you pray and ask the Holy Spirit to be your teacher, you will not gain the prophetic insight of what Elohim, the creator God, wants you to know about you and, most of all, about Him in you.

In 2010 the Holy Spirit spoke to us about the importance of the Tabernacle teaching and the impact it would have on the lives of believers, specifically those aspiring to be in leadership.

We have seen the manifested transformation of the lives of those who partake of learning to pray through the tabernacle. Each vessel and article in the temple is revealed to the leader in a threefold way, as themselves, as Jesus Christ, and what part each article plays in their relationship to God. As an example, the brazen altar represents how we must present ourselves as a living sacrifice, holy and acceptable to God which is our reasonable service.

Romans 12:1   A Living Sacrifice

[1] Therefore, I urge you, brothers and sisters, in view of God's mercy, to offer your bodies as a living sacrifice, holy and pleasing to God—this is your true and proper worship.

We teach how being a living sacrifice is an everyday occurrence of acknowledging sin, repenting, presenting oneself to God., placing ourselves upon the altar so that shortcomings and things that are not like God can be consumed.

We find that death becomes us as believers and definitely as leaders. The more you can put your will to death and allow the will of God to come alive, the more the health and wealth of a nation and a people will be revealed through you. In this way, God's vision and not man's will be revealed. The awesome concept about God's will is that He allows us, mere men, to ride on the wings of what He has established from the beginning of time. At times we get to be celebrated for what God has truly instituted. God is so giving that He allows us to partake of His Glory and to partner with Him in developing men and women He has called.

ONE ON ONE

ONE ON ONE

We call them love sessions. This is a time when the leaders in training come and talk one on one with the pastors concerning their life.

Connecting by intimate fellowship is a lost art. It is the piece in ministry that has fallen by the wayside and a time when you can allow a transference of thoughts to take place amongst a people. There is no hidden agenda and no set topic. The main theme of the session is to see where, how, and what is taking place in the life of the individual we are equipping for ministry. We realize that if you are not a whole person and not healthy in every area of your life, you will not be a good leader. You will not be balanced. We don't want to develop robots, but people who are able to identify with life's ups and downs and take time to address them. It makes for a touchable and approachable leader.

Many times people are lost in a crowd and pretend to be adjusting and learning in a church or group setting when they are in fact not connecting fully to what God wants to deposit into their lives. Sometimes it is the mere fact that there is a multitude of personal issues going on in their lives and they are not able to receive the fullness of the teaching going forth in the weekly events.

One on Ones allow us to evaluate the growth of the leader and to show them how amazingly God has brought them from one point to the next point. In addition, the quality time of listening to the leader's heart about certain issues pertaining to their teammates or just life in general is a very detoxifying and refreshing part of their development.

In the multitude of counsel there is safety. We are concerned about the individual leader and their ability to make Godly decisions on a daily basis. Being able to talk things out helps to eliminate much heartache and thought provoking time wasted on scenarios that may never play out.

Each leader is asked to meet at least every two or three months for a two hour minimal session. The one on one sessions are one of the most time consuming but powerful tools we use in developing the most effective leaders in Agape Time.

Below you will find a template that we use to keep a record and have a guide for the session. The template may, of course, be adjusted to meet any ministry's needs.

In addition we have couples sessions. These sessions are for couples who are in training together for leadership and for premarital counseling. What a challenge to be detoxified and developed for ministry while you are learning to walk with someone in life forever in marriage and also as a ministry teammate.

Every four months we have sessions of updates on what's happening—what has transpired for us as a ministry team and family. This is also a time when we discuss the circumstances if someone has abruptly left the ministry. I think it is really like having a flat tire and driving your car on three tires. If someone prematurely leaves the ministry, we talk about how it made their team members feel. As a group we must evaluate and talk about when something has changed.

HOUSE FELLOWSHIP

The fellowship seals the deal.

I don't know how many times we have heard leaders say, "When I walked in your house, I felt the love of God, I felt the peace of God, so I took my shoes off, and I wanna stay."

Even as I am writing this chapter my family room is filled with about ten young adults who have followed us home from Tuesday night Character Building class. We have a sectional, which seats seven people, a couch that seats three people, a love seat that seats two, an ottoman that seats three people, and a huge floor that seats as many as can find space to lie down, slump down, or sit down. They are laughing, eating, bonding, and connecting with one another and most of all God, in a different setting than church.

We find that in this atmosphere the leaders enter as strangers and leave as friends. The intimate yet relaxed situation helps in the interaction one with another. In this setting, the leader finds out two great truths.; "My pastors are real people and they really love God and me outside the church." They also find out and that fellow laborers in ministry have some of the same struggles and they are not alone.

The leaders love to ask Pastor John deep biblical questions and Pastor John loves to challenge them with late night trivia and thought provoking questions that make the leaders search their hearts and their bibles for the answers.

This environment is conducive to birthing the most profound conversations and most intriguing and in depth self examinations. One is able to let his or her guard down and get answers to life's questions whether it is how to deal with a boyfriend or girlfriend now that I am saved, to how to read my bible and understand what it is saying to me. We use this time as well to teach how to set up a teaching and/or preaching message or presentation.

The freedom we witness in those who partake of the house ministry is overwhelmingly successful. The deliverance is undeniable.

The leaders in training have coined the house fellowship as "real talk". Between the food, and the ole' so famous Motha Dillon's Tea, which the leaders in training named as well, it is the home fellowship that seals the deal.

Sabbath Rest

Many leaders who have come to the ministry have already been operating in some type of ministry for years. By the time they get to us, they are worn out and worn down,. They literally have nothing else to give and find it hard to receive because they are so worn down from entering in and out of venues, encountering and battling with demonic forces. While having no place to return to for retreat, restoration, and reload of spiritual armor. When they get to the house ministry they sleep for days.

The rest of God is a tangible feeling in the house. We have seen leaders literally transform into a different person inside and out. This need for rest from life and ministry that they were unaware of has come. Many do not know what to do with themselves. It is a time to settle down, discover one's self, analyze, life's past present, and future. It is a time to be detoxified, be delivered, be healed, and discover the most profound thing which is who they are in Christ Jesus.

Big Fun

Yes we have big fun! We cook together, eat together, and wash dishes together. We have all things common. Nothing is lacking. We have down time where we develop team skills by everyday chores. We have game time and chop it up sessions where we just jones on each other. That means cut up and make healthy fun of one another's jesters, character traits and presentations. It is done all in love and we have a Holy Ghost blast laughing and cutting up. Balance is the key to successful ministry and life.

We go bowling and enjoy other recreational things together. Everyone's birthday is celebrated in the ministry. Pastor John and I buy a small individual gift for each leader which is up to 70 leaders as of the writing of this manual and we intend to keep this one on one fellowship going and to impart into the leaders and allow it to flow downward where everyone is touched on a personal basis. Touching twenty percent always who touch the other eighty percent.

After all this, the time comes to go home. This means don't call me, don't text me and don't email. It is called downtime. No ministry . . . I mean no ministry. Pastor John and I take an away trip at least every six months because ministry is so intense for us. People come home with us every night, people live with us on an ongoing basis and we seem to be in counseling twenty four seven. All good, but not all healthy if you continue this with no breaks and no quality time for one another. Newlyweds in our ministry cannot come to the ministry for at least a month after getting married. Some are begging to come back before then but it is the House rule that newlyweds get to know one another even more and consummate, the marriage because once you come back to ministry, there will be a lot of sharing of your spouse with others.

Take care of your house, your spiritual house, and your spouse's spiritual house. Make sure the person you love and the leaders you develop are healthy on the inside. Peter says *I am building you up to be a spiritual house. And we must be a strong tower in the days to come.*

CHARACTER BUILDING— TRAINING BY DOING

CHARACTER BUILDING—TRAINING BY DOING

On Tuesday night you can walk into ATMI and see someone other than Pastors Dillon teaching the class. It is phenomenal to witness the creativity, and the presentation in which these leaders teach their class. Many of them are presenting a topic for the first time before people.

We are firm believers that if you don't have great character and integrity, your gift can only take you so far and you will be exposed by lack of character. Someone coined the phrase that "your gift will take you places that your character can't keep you."

I asked the Lord what would be the most accelerated pace to impart Godly character. He stated by the student or leader studying character, teaching it as a lesson, to others, and then living it out amongst his or her peers. The best way for the leaders to receive was to receive this particular teaching from one another. This would bring accountability, respect, and a healthy challenge.

Each team member is given a character trait such as *longsuffering* or *loyalty*. We also teach from the *"John Maxwell "21 Irrefutable Laws. "*They are given a six month advance notice of their teaching assignment. During this time frame., they have the opportunity to come and sit with Pastor John or myself and learn the techniques of putting a lesson plan together how to hear from the Lord, how to stand before a class room and how to capture the audience. The dynamics of this technique of giving the servant leader the challenge of teaching after the first five months is rewarding to the mentors and the mentees.

After teaching a character building class, the teacher does not have to walk away wondering if he or she was successful. At the end of every presentation, the teammates give the teacher positive feedback of insight gained, revelation received, how the class made them feel. Pastor John and I give verbal feedback as well. The feedback is always uplifting and inspiring. Each teacher for the evening is also given a written feedback as you will find in the manual by Pastor John. I have attached some of the lessons prepared by the students/leaders in training on Tuesday night. They are phenomenal.

SATURDAY
LEADERSHIP CLASS

SATURDAY LEADERSHIP CLASS

Make your calling and your election sure. (2 Peter 1:10)

11:30 a.m. every Saturday morning. Come with your spirit man open to receive the most profound impartation on a subject that many have quickly skipped over in Sunday school class. A subject that many leaders have ignored or seemly have thought develops within you without direction, guidance or teaching. One would be the gift of the Holy Spirit, the five-fold ministry gifts to the church and the charisma gifts.

Pastor John teaches on Saturday mornings. On the first and third Saturdays he takes each fivefold ministry gift. The Apostle, Prophet, Evangelist, Pastor and Teacher. He takes an in depth look at the character traits of each office. He meticulously delves into the personality of each. He makes the clear distinction as to whether you stand in the office of either of these or if you have the anointing. This is a major distinction that many miss which has led to people not walking in their lane as a leaders. It is major. Leaders who have been in ministry for years come to the class and find out that they really have never been a pastor but have been an evangelist and thereby become very relieved and effective.

Pastor John also takes that charisma gifts in Corinthians dissects and explains them with clarity.

We do prophetic demonstrations. Each office takes a six week period to examine what it looks like, what it feels like, and life's trials that you go through to attain the prize of a high calling in Christ Jesus.

On second and fourth Saturdays, Pastor John teaches on the Origin of the Holy Spirit. It is amazing to learn just how many people don't really know where the Holy Spirit originates, His attributes, and His operation. It is the Ruach HaKodesh, the breath of God and the very wind that is blown into man. Oh my! I can't talk about this subject without getting excited. I am thrilled every time I go to class to partake of Pastor John's teaching on the Holy Spirit. It never gets old. I have listened to him teach on the Origin of Holy Spirit for over 8 years. Not once have I been bored. In fact, it elevates yearly as the God gives reveals deeper insight and wisdom.

Pastor John teaches so eloquently yet he is so approachable and engaging clad normally in his baseball cap and throwback Cardinal or Rams jersey. He makes the, class palatable yet it is so intriguing. Though completely unintentional, sometimes the lessons can even seem intimidating, but with Godly reverence, as to what is housed in your body . . . The Holy Ghost.

It is undeniable that the Saturday classes, equips leaders to operate in their gifts and callings in the earth.

Usually there is a time for exercising what you have learned and to provide lots of feedback. Most of all, this is a time to realize that your "Life is Power in Motion." . . . Pastor John Dillon.

See below some of the handouts that can be used to teach the Origin of the Holy Spirit and Five Fold Ministry. Some of the content has been pulled from the Hebraic perspective which Pastor John has studied for over 25 years before releasing it to the world. Some are from other great men and women of God . . . who have written on the subject in depth and we have compiled a lesson plan from their efforts.

EXPRESSION SUNDAY

The chairs in the sanctuary have been moved out of the intimate circle set for Monday night prayer and into traditional church formation or theatre style. I like the theatre style description best. It betters describes what is about to take place. On Expression Sunday the leaders who have been trained all week, sometimes unawares, through prayer, character building class, Saturday leadership, and outside events, are now preparing to make their showing to the world. It is their debut of the many expressions or gifts that God has given them.

Expression Sunday is twofold. In a controlled environment, Pastor John and I help leaders to exercise their gifts under the direction of the Holy Spirit. Although the environment is controlled, it is freedom in the Holy Spirit. Those who attend as guests or family members are not aware that it is a training session, because the atmosphere is charged with the celebration of a risen King of Kings. The weighty presence of the Lord and His love is tangible. Those who partake of Expression Sunday return again and again.

On Expression Sunday the Holy Spirit gives the topic. The topic is derived from what is going on in the lives of the leaders at the present moment. It is prophetically inspired and heavenly fulfilled. The topics given are as such:" Firmly Planted Produces Fruit. "or "When Passion Meets Purpose" and "The Overcomers Anointing". The leader given the assignment as well as the rest of the team are able to discern that God is prophetically speaking in their now and in their future.

Expression Sunday allows the leader to become skilled in identifying different types of spiritual activity whether it is demonic hindrance or Holy Spirit led.

It helps the leader to actively discern what they see in the spirit realm while at the same time performing their God given task or assignment for the day.

A testimony we are always excited to tell is the one of Tyrone Nolan, who is now one of the Gatekeepers of Prayer. Tyrone came to Agape Time Ministries in July of 2010. He came from a background of gang affiliation and no religious background. He was saved filled with the Holy Spirit on the same day we met him. Now, he is a son of the house with incredible teaching ability, a warrior in the spirit, and awesome team player. His expression of pure prayer is amazing to behold and partake. After two years of walking with Tyrone until Christ was formed in him. He has developed into a trusted leader, a pillar of the house, and armor bearer to Pastor John. In addition he has birthed his own personal ministry, Warrior's Path.

It is a grieving exisitence to be developed or trained and never able to express.

AWAY ASSIGNMENTS

The Leader is now revealed to the world. It is now time for your showing. After the leader has attended Monday night prayer on the tabernacle he or she has been detoxified, refueled and given direction. Tuesday night class has helped to build the leader's character through teaching and being taught. Through lessons learned during Saturday class he or she now knows who they are in God and where their anointing flows. The leader has exercised, in a controlled environment, his or her gift amongst peers, family and friends. Now the leader is equipped for an away assignment.

The Leader is ready to go out, under supervision, to a ministry assignment. Many times Pastor John and I are called upon to speak and minister in conferences and church services. We take the whole team. Everyone is put to work Whether as an armor-bearer, an administrator, an altar worked or a person managing the product table, everyone is given an assignment. All leaders know they have to be ready because we may decide that he or she is the speaker that day in our stead. It is exciting. We prophesy in teams of three. In this way, an entire church can be ministered to in a matter of minutes and not hours as is often the case in a one man show. However, if it takes hours for us to walk a person out of a stronghold until deliverance comes; we can do that as well.

After an away assignment the leader is asked to complete spiritual assessments to begin to identify what they saw in the spirit in the service or meeting. They are asked to identify spiritual gifts such as the gift of the Leader in the house, which are the intercessors and so on. You can find the spiritual assessment attached. We have two types; one is for in town assignments and one is for out of town assignments.

The assessment must be submitted within a week after the event or away assignment. This technique helps to develop the spiritual insight as well as equip the leader in understanding atmosphere and what is really going on in any given service or meeting. WE are not just having church or going to preach. We are going to create a new atmosphere and to Stir Up the Gift of God in His people. You must have a trained eye to see what is happening in the atmosphere above you, around you, and before you while delivering a message of hope and revelation.

It has been prophesied that we will raise up a swat team that will take over territory, go into churches and bring deliverance, much needed freedom to believers, and set the captives free. This team will also bring revelation, sight to the blind, and apprehend that spirit that has troubled a camp of believers for years and assassinate that spirit of hopelessness and bring life where death was hovering.

Away, the Leaders go into their callings and elections, moving by the spirit and in the spirit. They have launched the lives in God to move and live and have their being in the most powerful life they could ever live.

When we return from an away assignment or execute an assignment in house there is a debriefing. During the debriefing each team member is able to express what was learned during the assignment. John and I have a list of particular tasks that were accomplished and not accomplished. We discuss as a team, what we could have completed better. Our goal in each assignment is to complete it with the excellence of Christ Jesus.

Forms we Use in the Ministry. You may adjust these to your own format. These are simple guidelines to get you started with developing your Team of Leaders.

TRAINING FORMS
YOU CAN USE

AGAPE TIME MINISTRIES—LEADERSHIP
Out of Town Spiritual Assessment

NAME: _____ DATE: _____
DESTINATION: _____
NAME OF CHURCH: _____
PASTORS NAME: _____

1) Prepare a time line of the whole trip.

2) What did you sense in the departing Prayer, and how were you feeling?

3) As we left the St. Louis area did you sense any change in the Spiritual environment?

4) When we passed through different towns and Spiritual regions could you sense a different atmosphere? (Explain each answer)
   a. Did you notice anything on the highway that defined part of that region?
   b. Could you tell if that region belong to G-d?

5) How many churches did you see on the way? Give Names

6) Could you sense any demonic or Angelic forces in operation? (How do you know that is what you were sensing)?

7) At each stop what was the atmosphere and could you sense any Christians in the Place?

8) When we reached the destination what was the atmosphere of the area?

9) What was the name of the church?

10) Did you sense the presence of the Lord during the message?

11) What was the main theme and focus of the message?

12) Name three spiritual gifts of the speaker? {Each Night}
    a.
    b.
    c.

13) When you first walked in the Church, what was the atmosphere like?

14) What was the spiritual atmosphere in the sanctuary? (Did you sense the presence of the Holy Spirit)

15) What is the vision of the Church?

16) Was the spirit of love present in the members?

17) Did you sense that the members had the heart of the Pastor?

18) During worship what was the atmosphere and was it true worship?

19) Were the worship leaders anointed?

20) Were the worship leaders able to usher you into the presence of the Lord? If not, what was the problem? Would you consider that church to be a safe place for the people of God and why?

21) How did the church and message affect your walk with God?

22) What did you sense during the altar call?

23) Did you recognize who the intercessors were and the true prayer warriors?

24) If you were going to exhort the speaker, what would you say to him/ her and why?

SPIRITUAL ASSESSMENT QUESTIONS

In-town

1. What was the name of the Church and what just recently happened?

2. What was the name of the speaker?

3. Did you sense the presence of the Lord during the message?

4. What was the main theme & focus of the message?

5. Name three of the spiritual gifts of the speaker.
   a.
   b.
   c.

6. When you first walked in the Church what was the atmosphere like?

7. What was the spiritual atmosphere in the sanctuary? (Did you sense the presence of the Holy Spirit)

8. Who were the Pastors or leaders and what were their names?

9. What was the vision of the Church?

10. Was the spirit of love present in the members?

11. During worship what was the atmosphere and was it true worship?

12. What were the children doing and why?

13. Were the worship leaders anointed?

14. Were the worship leaders able to user you into the presence of the Lord? If not what was the problem?

15. Would you consider that church to be a safe place for the people of G-d and why?

16. How did the church and message affect your walk with G-d?

17. What did you sense during the altar call?

18. Did you recognize who the intercessors were and the true prayer warriors?

19. If you were going to exhort the speaker what would you say to Him or Her and why?

ATMI LEADERSHIP CLASS TEACHER EVALUATIONS

DATE: _____

TEACHER: _____

SUBJECT: _____

1. Was the Leader on time and prepared to teach?

2. Was it apparent that the Leader studied the subject?

3. Did the Leader make a connection with the listeners?
    3.1. Were they able to bring the listeners back when they disconnected?

4. Did the Leader effectively involve the listeners?
    4.1. All of the Group
    4.2. Allow them to voice their opinions even if they disagreed with Leader?
    4.3. Allow the others to hold discussions and were fair in allowing everyone to speak?

5. Did the Leader capture and keep the attention of the Leaders?

6. Were there any visual aids and were they used effectively?
    6.1. Use of Dry ease board
    6.2. Any props

7. Was the use of personal stories effective or was their too many?

8. Did the Leader stick to the subject at hand or stray a lot from the original subject.

9. Were there any questions posed to the listeners?

10. Did the Leader effectively Facilitate and control the discussion?

11. Was the Leader showing confidence in the subject matter when they were teaching?

12. What was the reaction of the class after the presentation was over?

RECOMMENDATIONS:

AGAPE TIME MINISTRIES INC.—DEBRIEFING

Date: March 20, 2012—These observations were made during Healing Communities and Daughters Retreat held at the ATMI facility.

The Gate & Check In/Gatekeepers

- Standing with back to the Door
- Clutter at the Door
- Registration List Not always readily available
- Not showing guest to the next stage of registration
- During Healing Communities did not lead ppl to meet and greet area.
- Did not always if quest were ministers or clergy
- Did not always put offering buckets out.

Sanctuary

- Coats and purses—bags lying everywhere and on couches
- Leaders standing around talking instead of attending to task or assisting visitors
- Intercession did not go forth @ 6pm. Nightly
- Too much walking during service

Office—Pastors

- People gathering in office that are not authorized
- Office sometimes Not cleaned from night before

Product Table

- Not always manned
- Product not always prepared for sale/laying items on the product table (purses, water bottles, notebooks, etc.)
- Did not have prepared change
- No inventory count

Hospitality & Kitchen

- Did not wear purchased aprons
- Food presentation not acceptable all days—when Director was not present (i.e. Sandwiches in white container not cut nor was pickle—no sheet paper
- Items presented on to low of a table-
- Over prepared food—may need to wait for actual count on some days

Floor Administrators

- Not always on time
- Not sure of other leaders duties—did not print out administrative assignments
- Need to give more training on receiving offering

Altar

- Sometimes congested—did not move traffic through
- Catcher a little late
- Tissue not readily available some nights
- Not sure all the time when to remove chairs and furniture
- Not always focused and attentive

Sound Tech

- Not always attentive & prepared for what was to happen next with music selection
- Sometimes played music too low for dancers
- Did not order CD's in timely manner
- Did not go through proper protocol to order CD and inform leadership of cost and payment

Worship Team

- Not always on time
- Did not always have sound check

Armor Bearers

- Not always sure of position or what to do.
- Did not always bring guest speaker to office
- Sometimes Pastor P was not covered—even though assigned a AB

Financial Ministry

➢ Money not counted nightly & Count more expeditiously
➢ Some money left outside locked drawer—left on floor in bucket
➢ Unauthorized staff in office afraid to direct them out.

Bathrooms

➢ Not restocked nightly with tissue
➢ Some personal clothing items left on floor
➢ Not always cleaned from night before

Public Relations

➢ Welcome bags not available
➢ Did not always Engage newcomers give card and bag

EXPRESSION SUNDAYS FLOWS

EXPRESSION SUNDAY--------------------MARCH 25, 2012

TOPIC: FIRMLY PLANTED PRODUCES FRUIT

That person is like a tree planted by streams of water, which yields its fruit in season and whose leaf does not wither—whatever they do prospers. Psalms 1:3

Flow Sheet

Welcome/Prayer . . . Sharon Nolan

Worship Experience . . . ATMI Worship Team

Introduction of Pastors . . . Sharon-Nolan

Prophetic Proclamation . . . Pastors John & Pamela

Ministry of Arts . . . Prophetic Expressors

Since I been Planted . . . Tyrone Nolan

Ministry of Giving . . . Ischa Gibson

Prophetic Snapshot . . . Theresa Tompkins

Introduction of Speaker . . . Jeremiah Wells

Speaker . . . Kathy McClenton

Altar Call—Agape Time—Ken David Rose

EXPRESSION SUNDAY--------------------APRIL 22, 2012

For the weapons of our warfare are not carnal, but mighty through
God to the pulling down of strong holds II CORINTHIANS 10:4

Flow Sheet

Welcome/Prayer . . . Ischa Gibson

Worship Experience . . . ATMI Worship Team

Introduction of Pastors . . . Pamela Wilson

Prophetic Proclamation . . . Pastors John & Pamela

Ministry of ArtsProphetic Expressers

I released My Weapon of Faith & Love . . . Morene Williams

Ministry of Giving . . . Evang Sherri County

Prophetic Snapshot . . . Kristy Eason

Introduction of Speaker . . . Sharon County

War Cry . . . Theresa Tompkins

Speaker . . . Tyrone Nolan
Altar Call—Agape Time—Jaron Simon

- **Spiritual Gifts The Gift of the Holy Spirit:**

  - The Holy Spirit given to every believer upon salvation after accepting Jesus as Lord and Savior
  - Acts 2:38 the indwelling or baptism of the Holy Spirit, to seal you as a Child of G-d.

- **The Gifts of the Holy Spirit:**

  - Those abilities and capacities G-d gives that fit His plan and purpose for your Life

- **The Fruit of the Holy Spirit:**

  - The Character the Holy Spirit intends to build into each of our lives as we submit to His will and sovereignty, which allows us to walk in His will and His way. Galatians 5:

- **A spiritual gift will naturally use the talents that G-d gave to you when you were born.**

  - G-d intends for you to exercise both gifts to G-d's glory and our good
  - For the edifying of the Body of Christ

- **Three List of Categories of Spiritual Gifts: I Corinthians 12:7**

  - Equipping Gifts
  - Edifying Gifts
  - Evidence Gifts

- **Seven Motivational(Gifts of the Father) Gifts: Romans 12:5-8, Ephesians 4:11-12**

  - Prophecy
  - Leading/ Organization
  - Teaching
  - Exhortation
  - Service/Helps
  - Mercy
  - Giving

ATMI LEADERS COUNSELING
ONE ON ONE SESSION

ATMI "City of Refuge"

NAME:
MEMBER ATMI: yes   CHURCH MEMBERSHIP: ATMI "City of Refuge"
SESSION SUBJECTS: Monthly 1 on 1

PROGRESS NOTES:

Beginning Emotional State:

SESSION DATE: 7/ 2011

1) General & Spiritual Well Being:
   a)
   b)
   c)
   d)
   e)

2) Personal Issues:
   a)
   b)
   c)
   d)
   e)

3) Identify growth since you have been here:
   a)
   b)
   c)
   d)
   e)

4) Things we could make ATMI more affective:
   a)
   b)
   c)
   d)
   e)

5) Important Information:
   a)
   b)
   c)
   d)

AGAPE TIME MINISTRIES INC.—CITY OF REFUGE

Saturday—Leadership Training

Gift of the Holy Spirit & Gifts of the Holy Spirit—Series

A.) Origin of Holy Spirit:

    a)   Breath of G-D (Rauch HaKodesh) Genesis 1:1-5)
        i.   Job 27:3, Psalm 104:29, Job 34:14-15
    b)   Wind that cause motion in the Hebrew Letters (Torah)
    c)   Power of G-D in earth and heaven, glory/Authority of G-D
    d)   "The Lord our G-D is One" Shema
        i.   Triune vs. Trinity
        ii. Hellenistic Teachings
    e)   Same Spirit in the Old and New Testament
        i.   Isaiah 6:9, Acts 28:25-26
        ii. Jeremiah 31:33, Hebrews 10: 15-16

B.) **Who Is The Holy Spirit:**

    a)   **All the attributes of G-D:**
        i.   Eternal (Hebrews 9:14)
        ii.   Omniscient (Corinthians 2:10)
        iii. Omnipotent (Luke 1:35)
        iv. Omnipresent (Psalms 139: 7-8)
        v.   Majestic and Holy
        vi. Person of Action
        vii. Person of Administration
    b)   **Has Personal Actions:**
        i.   Holy Spirit Speaks (Revelation 2:7)
        ii.   Helps us un our infirmities/weaknesses (Romans 8:26)
        iii. Our Intercessor (Romans 8:26)
        iv. Teacher (John 14:26)
        v.   Testifies of the Lord (John 15:26)
        vi. Guides us (John 16:13)
        vii. Commands People (Acts 16:6-7)
        viii. Calls believers and appoints them to office

C.) Concerning Spiritual Gifts:

All of the gifts are supernatural gifts, not natural gifts
    viii. You cannot acquire them by going to a school and learning them, they do not come from you.
    ix. You cannot explain the work of the spiritual gifts as a talent you may posses
    x. You must confess your sins and be born again.
    xi. You must have received the Baptism of the Holy Spirit and continually be filled
    xii. Understand you are a vessel through which the gifts flow-the gift is not your own.
    xiii. We are to be reflectors of G-D's glory
    xiv. Gifts are not a sign of how spiritual you are
    xv. Gifts operate as the Spirit of G-D wills, and you must operate under the unction or anointing of the Spirit of
    xvi. G-D
    xvii. Must be a yielded vessel by which you yield your members so he can flow through us.
    xviii. Cannot take credit when G-d uses you, your motive are important when operating in the Spirit of G-D.

D.) Edification, Exhortation, and Comfort:

A. G-D never placed the Gifts in the Church to pull the Church down
B. Edification (rebuke, direction, correction, guidance, gird up)
C. Exhortation(joy, uplift, release, advocate, encouragement)
D. Comfort (console, consult)
E. Love must be your motive and a pure heart, and a desire to see the people of G-D blessed

E.) Diversities and Differences

A. I Corinthians 12:4" diversities of Gifts but same Spirit"
B. "Differences of administration but same Lord" vs.5
C. "Diversities of operation, but it is the same G-D which worketh all in all
D. G-D does not move the same all the time
E. G-D created change but he changes not
F. We are all unique in our ways, your personality, nature and character G-D will use who you are.

F.) Common Mistakes

1. **Don't** run around chasing miracles, prophecy
2. If you are not living a holy life, you may yield to the wrong spirit and be used of the devil.
3. Don't criticize what you don't understand or have never seen before.
4. Become an oracle of G-D, not an echo of man
5. Don't totally depend on your emotions or five senses when it comes to the things of G-D.

G.) Keys To Operating in the Gifts:

1. All gifts operate as G-D wills them to operate
2. You must have faith for the gifts to operate in you
3. Love for G-D and the people of G-D must be first and for most (I Corinthians 13:1)
4. Operation of the Gifts work under the anointing of G-D (always wait on the anointing)
   Always be sensitive to the Spirit of G-D (gifts don't operate in the mental or carnal realm) You must hunger and thirst after the things of G-D
5. obedience is one of the keys to operating under the anointing

1) Wisdom

1. **Wisdom**—is knowledge, understanding, experience, discretion, and intuitive understanding along with a capacity to apply these qualities well towards finding solutions to problems; it is the judicious and purposeful application of knowledge that is valued in society. To some extent the terms wisdom and intelligence have similar and overlapping meanings. The status of wisdom or prudence as a virtue is recognized in cultural, philosophical and religious sources.

2. Wisdom—(Chochmah)—Hebrew Knowing the way of the righteous-truth and justice.
   A. Perfection of the intellect
   B. The proper choice between two opposites-course of action
   C. Chochmah is the primary (beginning) force in the creative process, as it is said:" You have made them all with chochmah." The first word of the Torah, Breishit, "In the beginning,(God created the heavens and the earth), is translated as "with chochmah (God created)
   D. Cannot gain through your own intellect
   E. In Rabbi Aryeh Kaplan's commentary on the Bahir he says, "Wisdom (Chochmah) is therefore the first thing that the mind can grasp, and is therefore

called a 'beginning' Chochmah refers to "the first power of conscious intellect within Creation."

3. Wisdom—(Sophia—sofeeah) (Greek)
    1) Practical wisdom, prudent skill, comprehensive insight, Christian enlightenment, a right application of knowledge, insight into the true nature of things.
    2) Sophia (Greek for "wisdom") is a central theme or term in Hellenistic philosophy and religion, Platonism, Gnosticism, Orthodox Christianity, Esoteric Christianity, as well as Christian mysticism. Sophiology is a philosophical concept regarding wisdom, as well as a theological concept regarding the wisdom of God. Wisdom—(Jack Hay fords Study Bible)The ability to judge correctly and follow the best course of action, based on knowledge and understanding Classical views of wisdom, which sought through philosophy and man's rational thought to determine the mysteries of the existence and the universe.
        A. Wisdom of G-d (I Corinthians 1:18-25
        B. Wisdom of this world (I Corinthians 1:20, 3:19)
        C. Human Wisdom (I Corinthians 2:5)
        D. Wisdom of this age (I Corinthians 2:6)
        E. Man's wisdom (I Corinthians 2:13)

2) **Things of the Spirit: (Pneumatika)**

    A. **The "Pneumatika" and the New Testament.** In the letters of Paul we find the pneumatika of the New Testament. Reading the original Greek we might observe that Paul uses two words to refer to the gifts of the Holy Spirit: one is pneumatika (which comes from pneuma, Spirit), and the plural is pneumatikos, which means "the things that belong to the Spirit," the other one is charisma(this comes from charis, grace, gift) and its plural is charismata, and means a present or "gift of grace."
    B. **Examples of the word pneumatica. Greek word. Concerning spiritual gifts** I do not want you to be ignorant (I Corinthians 12:1) Since you are zealous for **spiritual gifts,** let is be for the edification of the church(1 Corinthians 14:12). Pursue love and desire spiritual gifts (I Corinthians 14:1). We speak in words which the Holy Spirit teaches, comparing **spiritual things** with spiritual (I Corinthians 2:13. This is a difficult text, and the form of pneumatika is adjective). The natural man does not receive the things of the Spirit of God (I Corinthians 2:14). Only one Greek word, pneumatikos, or one of its derivatives, says it all.
    C. **Conclusion from these examples.** From the study of these examples we conclude that pneumatica always refers to the things belonging to the Spirit, like an

action or something which serves as an instrument of the Spirit; or manifests the presence of the Spirit, Pneumatika is more generic; The pneumatika is the gifts or **gifts of the Spirit in general,**

3) **Spiritual Gifts (Charismata)**

    a)   Paul uses two basic words for what are normally called "spiritual gifts." The first, Charisma (plural—Charismata) occurs 17 times in the New Testament and rarely in Greek literature outside the New Testament. It does not even occur in the Greek version of the Old Testament, the Septuagint.

    a)   But the word as commonly used today has the limited connotation of a special gift or manifestation of the Spirit granted to individuals for the edification of the congregation (Romans 12:6;, 1 Corinthians 12:4,9,28,30,31). Paul tells the Corinthian Christians they are not lacking in any charisma (1 Corinthians 1:7)

    b)   Both charismata and pneumatika are used in parallel statements; "Covet earnestly the best gifts (Charismata) (1Corinthians 12:31) and, "Desire spiritual gifts {pneumatika}" (14:1)

    c)   The words therefore are used interchangeably. But based on the root meaning of each, charismata emphasizes that they are gifts of the Spirit; pneumatika emphasizes that they are gifts of the Spirit, They are neither earned nor humanly generated.

As an apostolic house whom births out spiritual sons and daughters. We intensely train and equip leaders for the five-fold ministry anointing. Providing the leader has heard the call as an individual. Although we may know their gifting by the Holy Spirit we skillful train them in the area in which they are called. Sometimes this training and equipping is unbeknownst to them. Leaders are not encouraged to focus on any particular gift. As all leaders are taught the mannerism, protocols, spiritual understanding of them all. This makes for a pure election of the Lord and not a man made choice. The ministry gifts to the church found in **Ephesians 4:11-15 King James Version (KJV).**

[11] And he gave some, apostles; and some, prophets; and some, evangelists; and some, pastors and teachers; [12] For the perfecting of the saints, for the work of the ministry, for the edifying of the body of Christ:[13] Till we all come in the unity of the faith, and of the knowledge of the Son of God, unto a perfect man, unto the measure of the stature of the fulness of Christ: [14] That we henceforth be no more children, tossed to and fro, and carried about with every wind of doctrine, by the sleight of men, and cunning craftiness, whereby they lie in wait to deceive; [15] But speaking the truth in love, may grow up into him in all things, which is the head, even Christ:

Along with being taught the ministry gifts of apostles; prophets; evangelists; pastors and teachers; and the types of manifestations that come along with them. We teach how personality traits are sometimes synonymous with the developing and identifying gifting and calling.

We use the secular personality trait evaluation of choleric, sanguine, melancholy, and phlegmatic. It makes for a very interesting, fun, and to say the least eye opening behaviors that really do fit many of our behaviors. As we learn the different behaviors of each individual and their calling in the earth. We learn how to unite and work together. Most of all we begin to understand our fellow co laborers, what makes them tick and how to work alongside them in the kingdom of God.

SOME OF THE STUDENTS HANDOUTS FOR CHARACTER BUILDING CLASS

The Law of Solid Ground

Leader In Training—Teacher: Jeremy Eason

1. **Set The Stage (John 4)**
   1.1. Jesus' starting point, route, and destination are a picture of the maturity of a leader.
      a) He begins in Jerusalem which is in situated in Judea. Jerusalem represents knowledge becoming ritual.
         - Jesus was there for Passover
         - What had begun as a celebration of G-D's mercy became a ritual that determined righteousness.
            - Don't let what you learn about G-D become something you are forced to do in order to be right with G-D.
         - Their appearance became the measuring stick for their relationship rather than their hearts.
      b) He is then forced to go through Samaria in order to get to his destination. Samaria is characterized by hills and valleys in perfect balance designed to test character. (Job 31:6). Where what you think you learned is challenged (challenged; not proved wrong).
         - Samaria is a rocky region that literally means "mountain of watching" or "guardianship".
         - Most Jews would have avoided Samaria all together. The "religious" don't choose to go through Samaria.
         - Samaritans challenged the assumed place of worship, the assumed acts of worship, and the assumed description of worship.
            - They worshiped on the mountain instead of in Jerusalem, they did not take part in the same rituals as the Jews, and they only used the Pentateuch and did not use the prophets or the writings.
         - Samaritans way of life asked questions that those in Jerusalem vehemently did not want to answer.
            - When experiences happen to you that you cannot explain by the knowledge you have obtained, it can bring frustration and anger if you are not willing to admit error and the possibility of not "knowing all things".

c) Jesus' destination was Galilee. Galilee represents the furthest from your religious comfort zone, but the closest to your value as a leader.
- Galilee was a mixed population of all kinds of people. The need for character is two fold. It allows those who may follow you to know that
- your outward appearance matches your inward appearance. And your character will guard you from compromise when exposed to the multitude of idols that come with the multitudes of people.
- Samaria prepares you to be able to minister to the multiple nations within Galilee.
- Galilee (the multitudes) is where true leadership is tested.

2. The Worship Leader
2.1. The ideas that are the Law of Solid Ground.
a) Character makes trust possible and trust makes leadership possible.
b) To build trust a leader must exemplify competence, connection, and character.
c) It's not the decisions, it's the leadership.
d) Trust must come before support.
2.2. Jesus Identifies the tenants of the Law of Solid Ground as identifies living water versus Jacob's well.
a) Jesus introduces the difference between his water and Jacobs well at a place called Sychar which brings with it the meaning of drunkenness, confusion, and perversion.
- Jesus offers his living water not because the regular water wouldn't quench her thirst, but because the living water would change her condition as well as her discomfort.
- Proverbs 25:26 states "A righteous man falling down before the wicked
- is as a troubled fountain, and a corrupt spring. This well of Jacob represents a lack of character within leadership.
- The situation shown her is that you can get things done without character but you can't change people. I can do church work without character but I can't do kingdom assignments.
- Jacobs water represents clean hands with a nasty heart. Good deeds that carry bad character.
2.3. Jesus Identifies the tenants of the Law of Solid Ground as he identifies worship.
a) Jesus arrives at Sychar (drunken) and he finds a woman there looking for water. He quickly initializes the process by which to create a situation where she can trust him.
- He brings a connection through allowing her to see that he is just as thirsty as she is. He asks her for a drink of water knowing that she also came for a drink of water. She also notices a connection between them in their relation to Jacob.

- He brings adequacy (competence) by proclaiming to her that he is in possession of what she needs with an added bonus. Not only does this
- water cure thirst but it has a component that affects life.
- He shows character when, in the person of a Jew, he doesn't approach her the same way the other Jews she had previously come in contact with would have. It is a pleasant surprise for a rejected person to not be rejected by someone that they assumed would reject them.

b) As Jesus demonstrates leadership he also deals with the leadership within the woman because the goal of a leader is not to gather followers but it is to make other leaders. He needs to create a situation now where she can be trusted by others.

- He deals with her character when he begins to question her about her husband. He does not initially accuse her but he asks a question that allows her to identify her own bad character and then he approaches it.
- He deals with her competence when he challenges her idea of worship. He doesn't necessarily challenge where she worships but what she worships because the idea is that if she knew what she worshiped then place would not be an issue. If she understood the omnipresence of G-D then worship would take on a different identity for her.
- He deals with her connection as he exclaims to her that G-D is spirit and her worship is determined by how she seeks to connect to him not where. In essence he allows her competence and character to generate a connection.
- When she leaves the presence of Jesus she immediately displays her support of him and her leadership by going into the city and directing people to him. Jesus got her trust and then her support.

Questions

1) Is the Lord addressing your character, your competence, or your connection?
2) Do you think people should support (endorse) you because of your position?
3) How much do people trust you?
4) Are you as ready for leadership as you thought you were? If not, can you see progression or digression?
5) Are you in Jerusalem, Samaria, or Galilee?
6) Do I do what I expect from others?
7) Do you treat your house like you treat G-d's house.
8) If I'm the same way everywhere, what do I need to work on?

The 21 Indispensable Qualities of A Leader

John C. Maxwell

CHARACTER: " Be a Piece of the Rock"

char·ac·ter: [kar-ik-ter]

—*noun*

1. the aggregate of features and traits that form the individual nature of some person or thing.
2. one such feature or trait; characteristic.
3. moral or ethical quality: *a man of fine, honorable character.*
4. qualities of honesty, courage, or the like; integrity: *It takes character to face up to a bully.*
5. reputation: *a stain on one's character.*
6. good repute.
7. an account of the qualities or peculiarities of a person or thing.
8. a person, esp. with reference to behavior or personality: *a suspicious character.*
9. *Informal.* an odd, eccentric, or unusual person.

adj.

Being a feature that helps to distinguish a person or thing; distinctive: *heard my friend's characteristic laugh; the stripes that are characteristic of the zebra.*

n. A feature that helps to identify, tell apart, or describe recognizably; a distinguishing mark or trait.

Moral character or **character** is an evaluation of a particular individual's <u>moral</u> qualities. The concept of *character* can imply a variety of attributes including the existence or lack of <u>virtues</u> such as <u>integrity</u>, <u>courage</u>, <u>fortitude</u>, <u>honesty</u>, and <u>loyalty</u>, or of good behaviors or <u>habits</u>.

Moral character primarily refers to the assemblage of qualities that distinguish one individual from another—although on a cultural level, the set of moral behaviors to which a social group adheres can be said to unite and define it culturally as distinct from others. Psychologist Lawrence Pervin defines moral character as "a disposition to behave expressing itself in consistent patterns of functioning across a range of situations" (Pervin 1994, p. 108).

The word **"character"** is derived from the Greek word *charaktêr*, which was originally used of a mark impressed upon a coin. Later and more generally, it came to mean a point by which one thing was told apart from others (Timpe 2007). There are two approaches when dealing with moral character: <u>Normative ethics</u> involve moral standards that exhibit right and wrong conduct. It is a test of proper behavior and determining what is right and wrong. <u>Applied ethics</u> involve specific and controversial issues along with a moral choice, and tend to involve situations where people are either for or against the issue (Timpe 2007).

In 1982, Campbell and Bond proposed the following as major factors in influencing character and moral development: <u>heredity</u>, early childhood experience, modeling by important adults and older youth, peer influence, the general physical and social environment, the communications media, what is taught in the schools and other institutions, and specific situations and roles that elicit corresponding behavior (Huitt 2004, §Impacting Moral and Character Development).

CHARACTER OF G-D

If it's true that God doesn't change and if you believe it with your whole heart, then, Beloved, you'll find yourself ready and able to handle every enemy that confronts you, every temptation that seeks to seduce you. You'll be prepared to go through trials and resist temptation as more than a conqueror. You won't need to panic. You'll be able to stand firm.

As I teach through the Old Testament, I am awed at what we can learn about God's character and how He deals with us if we only study this portion of Scripture. God gave us these precious books to teach us not only about Him but also about ourselves. Whether common people or kings, God expected men and women to live by His precepts because they are precepts for life and understanding (Psalm 119: 97-104).

    📖 89 (**Lamed**) Your word continues forever, ADONAI, firmly fixed in heaven;
         90 your faithfulness through all generations; you established the earth, and it stands.

91 Yes, it stands today, in keeping with your rulings; for all things are your servants.
92 If your Torah had not been my delight, I would have perished in my distress.
93 I will never forget your precepts, for with them you have made me alive.
94 I am yours; save me because I seek your precepts.
95 The wicked hope to destroy me, but I focus on your instruction.

God is *who* He has always been. He is immutable (1 Samuel 15:29; Malachi 3:6; Hebrews 6:18; James 1:17). He never changes; He's "the same yesterday and today and forever" (Hebrews 13:8).

(Kay Arthur)

- *Malachi 3:6 CJB*

  "But because I, ADONAI, do not change, you sons of Ya'akov will not be destroyed.

- *1 Samuel 15:29 CJB*

  Moreover, the Eternal One of Isra'el will not lie or change his mind, because he isn't a mere human being subject to changing his mind."

- *Hebrews 6:17 CJB*

  Therefore, when God wanted to demonstrate still more convincingly the unchangeable character of his intentions to those who were to receive what he had promised, he added an oath to the promise;

- *1 Peter 3:4 CJB*

  rather, let it be the inner character of your heart, with the imperishable quality of a gentle and quiet spirit. In God's sight this is of great value.

"Anyone who has seen Me has seen the Father!" John 14:9

"When he [any person] looks at Me, he sees the One who sent Me." John 12:45

"The Son is the radiance of God's glory and the exact representation of His being." Hebrews 1:3

PUTTING IT ALL ON THE LINE:

1) Bill Lear—inventor of Lear Jet
   a. Aviator, business leader, inventor
   b. More than 150 patents
      i. Automatic pilot
      ii. Car radio
      iii. Eight track tapes

2) 2 aircraft had crashed under mysterious circumstances
   a. 55 jets were privately owned
   b. Order the owners to ground aircraft at substantial loss of money
   c. Researched and discovered a potential cause
   d. Recreated the problem personally at risk to His own life

Fleshing It Out:

1) How a leader deals with circumstances of life tells you many things about his character
   a. Crisis doesn't necessarily make character, but it does reveal it.
   b. Adversity is a crossroads that makes a person choose one of two paths: character or compromise
   c. "The meaning of earthly existing lies, not as we have grown used to thinking, in prospering, but in the development of the soul." Nobel Prize winner Alexander Solzhenitsyn
   d. What must every person know about character?
      i. Character is more than talk
         1. You can never separate a leader's character from his actions
      ii. Talent is a gift, but Character is a choice
         1. We create our character every time we make a choice
      iii. Character Brings lasting Success with People
         1. True leaders always involve other people
      iv. Leaders cannot rise above the Limitations of Their Character
         1. Success Syndrome
         2. Arrogance, painful feelings of aloneness
         3. Destructive adventure seeking
         4. Idolatry

BRINGING IT HOME:

1) SEARCH FOR THE CRACKS:
   a. Look at majors areas of your life:
      i. Identify were you might have cut corners
      ii. Compromised
      iii. Let people Down
      iv. Disobeyed G-d

2) LOOK FOR PATTERNS:
   a. Weaknesses
   b. Problems that keep surfacing
   c. Detectable patterns
   d. Going thru the same trail

3) FACE THE MUSIC:
   a. Face your flaws
   b. Repent/apologize
   c. Deal with the consequences of your actions
   d. Don't blame others for your failures

4) REBUILD:
   a. Build a new future
   b. Create a plan that will keep you from making the same mistakes
   c. Ask G-d for help, and forgive yourself
   d. Seek wisdom from the Word of G-d to rebuild your character

John Maxwell   4-17-12

Law of Magnetism Part I

(Who You Are Is Who You Attract)

Definition

Magnetism-*a*: a class of physical phenomena that include the *attraction* for iron observed in lodestone and a magnet, are *inseparably* associated with *moving electricity*, are exhibited by *both magnets* and *electric currents*, and are characterized by *fields of force*.

John Maxwell definition of law of magnetism—"What you are is what you attract."

John Maxwell mentions . . .

EFFECTIVE LEADERS ARE always on the lookout for good people. He also says he thinks each of us carry around a mental list of what kind of people we would like to have in our organization. Think about it. Do you know who you're looking for right now? What is your profile of perfect employees? What qualities do these people posses? Do you want them to be aggressive and entrepreneurial? Are you looking for leaders? <u>What type of people do you want on your team?</u>

MY PEOPLE WOULD HAVE THESE QUALITIES

    1._____
    2._____
    3._____

FROM MUSICIAN TO LEADERSHIP

His predecessor at Skyline Church was Dr. Orval Buthcher man full of qualities. Dr. Orval had a solid reputation for fine music. Dr. Orval naturally attracted people with musical talents. They respected him and understood him. They shared his motivations and values. They were on the same page with him. After John came on board at the church, the numbers of musicians declined quickly. So what type of leaders came on board? Leaders. By the time he left Skyline, it was filled with leaders; the church also equipped and sent out hundreds of men and women as leaders! (ATMI)

A FEW KEY SIMILARITIES

Attitude

It's rare to see positive & negative people that are attracted to one another.

Generation

People tend to attract others of roughly the same age.

Background

Theodore R. attracted wealthy aristocrats & cowboys.

Values

People are attracted to leaders whose values are similar to their own.

Life Experience

Life experience is another area of attraction for people.

Leadership Ability

The people who you attract will have leadership ability similar to your own. If you are a 7 when it comes to leadership, you're more likely to attract 5s & 6s than 2s & 3s.

Law of Magnetism Part II

(Draw Nigh to God and He Will Draw Nigh to You)

James 4:8 <u>Draw nigh to God, and he will draw nigh to you</u>. Cleanse your hands, ye sinners; and purify your hearts, ye double minded.

What causes me to draw nigh to God? Answer: God, it's his spirit inside me that draws me back to him.

What causes me not to draw nigh unto God?

What are some of the filters (sins/ distractions) that keep you from not being close to God? What demagnetizes (disconnects) you from God?

Filter examples:

- Some are solid (strong holds)-black
- Some are shear (things your still struggling with)
- Some are clear but you can still see the out line of what it is but not the actual substance of what it is (things you've been delivered from, now you're able to help others).

Filters that keep you from seeing God

The more filters you have between you and your relationship with God the less closer you are with him. Sin keeps you away, but when you repent and turn from your sin, that puts you back in right standing with God. Although certain actions of sin has different consequences. You have to start building up that magnetic force field (reading your bible, worshiping, dying to the flesh and repenting to make you stronger in your walk with God, your drawn more to him and now he's drawn closer to you. Now you're more likely to follow after God and not be drawn away by sin and distractions (filters in life).

Filters Are There but You Can Still See God

When you have filters in your life that don't overshadow your relationship with God you can still see and hear God clearly. Your hunger for God grows, you start to realize the more you draw nigh to God he draws nigh to you! God is actually real and alive in your life, even when filters come along (bumps in the road) comes your way you know nothing can stop you from worshipping God. Some of the things you were once drawn to, you're no longer drawn to them, some people and things that were once drawn to you no longer have a magnet in you to attach itself to. Now you're able to help others let go of the filters that keep blocking them, ex. (un-forgiveness, bitterness, back biting, gossiping, doubting, fear etc.) from really knowing God and his character. Now your filters become full of life, character, repentance, forgiveness, love, patience with others and you're now full of compassion. Then . . . people not only see you, they start to see what's in you, what's around you, who's in you, they start to see God in you! They don't see the biggest solid filter blocking the light in you anymore. The filter might still be there, but the light of God is illuminating so bright in you, they only can see the outline (things from you past). Sometimes if people can't see you changing it's because they have filters in their own eyes.

Conclusion

The Law of Magnetism is always active. Sometimes if you don't like what's being drawn to you, ask God what it is in you that draw certain things or people in your life that you don't want. On the other hand it can be a process that you're going thru in order to begin to attract the pure and holy things of God to operate in your life.

Memory Scripture:

James 4:8 Draw nigh to God, and he will draw nigh to you. Cleanse your hands, ye sinners; and purify your hearts, ye double minded.

The end . . .

NOTES

_____

_____

_____

_____

_____

_____

_____

_____

_____

_____

_____

_____

_____

_____

_____

_____

_____

_____

_____

_____

Thank you!

WHO IS AGAPE TIME

WHO IS AGAPE TIME MINISTRIES INC.— CITY OF REFUGE AND WHAT DO THEY DO?

Who is Agape Time Ministries Inc.-City of Refuge and what do they do? After being asked this very question so often, we thought it proper, profitable, and respectable to respond to the Body of Christ with an answer. It is with great delight, and integrity that we introduce to some and present to others Agape Time Ministries Inc.-City of Refuge.

Agape Time Ministries (ATMI) is a God breathed ministry *that produces and promotes healthy leaders through mentorship and fellowship,* which is the active vision statement of this innovative and relational minded ministry. Agape Time was birthed into the earth in February of 1997 with the scripture Ezekiel 16:8: Now when I passed by you and looked upon you it was a time of Love, I made a covenant with you and you became mine. (paraphrased) Our sincere goal is to connect the believer with Christ in an intimate and personal way which leads to personal identity. In obedience to the call of the Lord, Pastors John & Pamela Dillon heard the turbulence in the atmosphere for Change. The mandate is to make ready a 24 hour worship center, multifaceted, multi-cultural, and interdenominational facility, which house diverse ministries, and offers respite for those in ministry. It is a safe place where every God-given gift can be stirred up and expressed. ATMI is a ministry that has church and we actively train the believer how to have healthy church or gatherings of the its believers.

ATMI humble beginnings began in Oklahoma City, Oklahoma where Pastor Pamela Dillon resided for many years. Pamela conceived the vision of "Stir Up the Gift" Summit in 1997 and out of those awesome summits many ministries and ministers were equipped, restored, revived, and refreshed for the next years mandate. Pamela was licensed and ordained into ministry in 1994 by her beloved Spiritual Father, Dr. Eddie O'Dell, pastor and founder of the House of Prayer Baptist Church and was launched into ministry and encouraged to complete her God given mandate. After many years of devotion to the House of Prayer as an Associate Minister. Pamela was called to support in leadership with Apostle Michael Johnson, Pastor of The Refreshing Church, one of the Worship Hubs of Oklahoma City for several years before moving to St. Louis, Missouri. Apostle Johnson covers, nurtures, protects, and fathers the Agape Time Ministries with respect, honor, and admiration.

A beautiful union and merger of ministries began in September of 2002 when Elder John Dillon of St. Louis, former member of the historical Kennerly Temple Church of God In Christ under the awesome leadership of Bishop R.J. Ward. John and Pamela married and became one in heart and spirit. Thus began the God ordained kinship of two hearts in ministry with like focus and same vision. John & Pamela went before the Lord once again to clearly hear the call for their lives as a *team*. Out of this prayer and consecration came the "City of Refuge" a facility that endeavor s to embrace, inspire, motivate, and equip men and women of God to pursue their callings in the earth. The voice of the Lord was loud, clear, and precise, to, build a house where, His Glory would remain perpetually where people of God could come and partake of the Divine presence of the True and Living God. A place where the body of Christ could safely dismantle their cares and receive a impartation from the Holy Spirit in Love.

Agape Time Ministries Inc, is a safe place that offers to leaders of all genders, denominations, races to come and partake of the prophetic atmosphere of prayer. A place where you can receive a fresh word. foundational, solid biblical teaching.

Agape Time is a gathering place for the people of God. John and Pamela are uncomplicated people who are more driven to develop the person, than erect bricks and mortar. Although it is a necessity, a need and of great biblical importance to have a gathering place the created man is first on their agenda. John and Pamela are very clear of their apostolic calling to produce, promote, and release leaders into their God given assignment. Also to be a confident to those who are seasoned in ministry and offer a refuge and respite.

Agape Time is a intense ministry whose passion is after the heart of God and to connect people of God with him in a manifested relationship. Those who are not sincere about entering into a true relationship with God the Father will not be moved by the flow of this ministry.

Are you sort of getting a picture of this kingdom minded mandate.

Agape Time's Kingdom Perspective:

Train Teams and to Promote Team Ministry. Anyone who Encounters Agape Time around St. Louis, we encounter the Team Anointing. They are usually in the same colors and come as a corporate group to produce the Glory and promote unity in any venue.

- Give each Ministry or Minister a platform to launch their gift with true support.
- Be networks and unifiers. To embrace other pastors in the community and their efforts to come along side as a support.
- Call Pastors and ministers from around the city and country in to teach and develop on any given subject

We offer:
- Leadership Development
- Mentorship
- One on One counseling
- Seminars
- Conference
- Round Table Summit
- Media Training
- Banner & Flag Ministry Training.
- 24 hour worship
- 3-7 day respite for those in ministry in any capacity.
- We offer in house training to ministry team, ie. altar workers, greeters, armor bearers, ministers in training.
- WE come to your venue train

Ministry Highlights:

"Stir Up The Gift Summit"—A gathering of 5 fold Leadership

"Intimate Evening with the Father"—An Extravagant evening of Prophetic Prayer, Worship, administer by Surrounding Area Pastors.

"Expression Sunday"—Every 4th Sunday—Leaders are given the opportunity ti Express their gift in what ever genere.

"Daughters Retreat"—Annual in March—A four day time of renewal, restoration, prophetic direction, encouragement for ATMI ministry daughters.

"Prophetic Expressers"—Agape Time Ministries—Dance, Mime, Banner, and Flag Team *"Wind Carriers & Daddy Dumplins"*—ATMI's Children's Ministries

After saying all of this, I know you are wondering, how can I join? How can I participate? There are several ways to partake of the Ministry.

"The S.P.O.T—St. Louis"—Speciliazing In the Potential of Teens & Young Adults-: Entertainment Center, Music Arts, After-school tutoring, and mentorship.

- You may become a bona fide team member and be trained and developed.
- You may come for training with written permission from you pastor—**you may not join**

- You may submit your ministry under the auspices of ATMI for training with Recommendations.
- You may Partake of our Monday night open prayer meetings, summits, and other sessions without being a member.

The types of ministries that are currently covered by Agape Time Ministries Inc. are not just traditional church ministries, but marketplace ministries.

- **First Fruits 2 Day LLC**—Founder, Ken David Rose—provides professional makeup for special events, individuals and celebrities.
- **Warriors Path Ministry**—Founder, Tyrone Nolan
- **Monique Renee Ministries**—Monique Renee Reynolds-Fulks is one who goes in and wars in the spirit realm through song. She moves the wind through sound. She is a recording artist.
- **Kevin Downswell**—Jamacian born, gospel recording artist . . . atmosphere changer and evangelist
- **Selah Music Network and Productions**-founder Tracy Jackson who brings artist together Untie, Restore, and Support.
- **Pastor Eva Natango**—Apostle to 70 churches in Africa
- **IMG—Ischa Marie Gibson**—Creative Image & Design Ministry

The list goes on in ministries

On a regular basis the following sessions are available:

Monday—7 pm	Praying Through the Tabernacle with Live Furnishings
Tuesday—7 pm	Leadership Training-Character Building
Saturday— 11:30 a.m.	Teaching on the Holy Spirit—Activations of the Gifts, Prophetic Training.
Monday-Thursday 10:30-5:00 pm.	One on One mentorship appointments
2nd & 4th Sunday—1:30 p.m.	Expression Sunday

Agape Time is a 501 (c) 3 non profit organization. All donations are tax deductible.

Endorsements of Powerful Men & Women of God.?

The American church communities at large is not absent of the many so called "ministries" that have been self-appointed and still wounded. While these ministries occupy a sincere mission to build greater dimension of themselves, they forget about the idea of building people for their ministry. Then you have ministries that have been called, proved, & sent. Their message is yet biblical, but their lives are formed with integrity and love. Pastors John & Pamela Dillon are humbled servants, anointed specialist and faithful supporters . . ." *Pastor J. Sims Word of Life Christian Church/ St. Louis, MO*

Pastors John & Pamela Dillon are one of the most loving couples I know. You are every bit of pastors after God's own heart. Everything that makes up a strong ministry, you two envelope . . . Pastor Michelle King . . . New Dimensions Church, East St. Louis, ILL

A great man of **God know around the city of St. Louis,** *Pastor Charles Roach* asked Pamela & John the question. "What makes you unique and what do you offer that sets you apart from other ministries that may be attempting to do the same thing." The answer was "on purpose we enter into a relationship with the leaders, true one on one mentorship, and encourage leaders to enter into a relationship with God and be led by the Holy Spirit. We ask every leader to leave their gift at the door, it is the heart and character God wants to develop . . .

What We Believe

Agape Time Ministries Inc.-City of Refuge—Belief and Vision Commitment

A Time of Love—

Ezekiel 16:8

When I passed by you and saw you again and looked upon
you, indeed your time was the time of love;

Agape Time Ministries Inc. City of Refuge: (ATMI) is a ministry with a heart after God and a heart for His people. Our mission is to equip the people of God through an intimate relationship with God for their kingdom assignments here on earth.

Our Vision Statement:

Producing & Promoting Healthy Leaders through Mentorship & Fellowship

The Word of God

Agape Time Ministries (ATMI) believes the scriptures to be the inspired Word of God without error in the original writings—the complete revelations of His will for the salvation of men and the final authority for all Christian faith and life. (2 Timothy 3:16-17, 2 Peter 1:19-21, Matthew 5:17-18, John 10:34-36)

The Triune God

ATMI believes in one God, creator of all things, infinitely perfect and eternally existing in three manifestations. God the Father, God the Son, and The Holy Spirit or Holy Ghost. *(Deuteronomy 6:4. Isaiah 9:6, Matthew 28:19, Romans 1:20, 2 Corinthians 13:14., Hebrew 1:1-3)*

The Father

ATMI believes in God the Father (Elohim-creator of all things), an infinite personal Spirit, perfect in holiness, wisdom, power, and love. We believe that He actively and mercifully intervenes in the affairs of men, that He hears and answers prayer, and that He save from sin and death all who come to Him through His Son Jesus Christ. *(Exodus 34:6-7, John 3:16, John 4:23-24, Ephesians 1:3)*

The Son

ATMI believes that Jesus the Christ (Yeshua ha Mashiach) is God and man. He was conceived by the Holy Spirit and born of the Virgin Mary. He lived a sinless life. He died on the cross as a sacrifice for our sins. He rose bodily from the dead. He ascended into heaven. He is now our High Priest and Advocate at the right hand of the Father. *(John 1:1-18, Colossians 1:15-23, Ephesians 1:15-23, Hebrews 2:23-25)*

The Holy Spirit

ATMI believes that the Holy Spirit is fully God and is the breath of God. We believe the Holy Spirit is equal with the Father and the Son. The Holy Spirit convicts unbelievers of their need for Christ; He gives new birth to believers, and He indwells, sanctifies, leads, teaches, and empowers believers for Godly living and service. We believe that the ministry of the Spirit continues to be a broad, tangible, and powerful among believers today as it was in the early church. We believe in the baptism of the Holy Spirit. We believe in speaking in tongues as the Holy Spirit gives utterance. We also believe that all the biblical gifts of the Spirit continue to be distributed by the Spirit today, that these gifts are divine provisions central to spiritual growth and effective ministry and that these gifts are to be eagerly desired, faithfully developed, and lovingly exercised according to biblical guidelines. *(John 3:3-8, John 14:15-27, John 16:5-15, Romans 8:9-17, Romans 12:3-*, I Corinthians 2:12-14, Galatians 5:16-26, Ephesians 5:18-21, I Corinthians 14: 1-25)*

Man

ATMI believes God created man in the image of God. We further believe man is a sinner by nature and action and is therefore spiritually dead. We also believed that those who repent of sin and trust Jesus Christ as Savior are spiritually born again to new life by the Holy Spirit.(Genesis 1:27, Ephesians 2:1-9, Romans3:9-26, Romans 5:12-21, Acts 2:38-39)

Salvation

ATMI believes that salvation is a free gift of God and is received by man through faith in Jesus Christ apart from any human merit, works, or ritual. We believe that the shed blood of Jesus Christ and His resurrection provide the only grounds for forgiveness of sins for all who believe and that only those who receive Jesus Christ are born of the Spirit, and are given eternal life. (Ephesians 2:4-9, Titus 3:5-7, Romans 3:21-31, John 3:16-17, Acts 16:29-34, Romans 10:9-10, John 8:23-24, John 14:6, I Timothy 2:3-6)

Water Baptism

ATMI believes in the submerging in water as a sign of your belief in the resurrected Jesus Christ. We believe that baptism in water identifies the believer with Jesus Christ, in his death, burial, and resurrection. Baptism expresses faith the way a word expresses an idea. Water baptism is a symbol of the spiritual union of Chris and the believer. We believe water baptism becomes a spiritual realities and vivid to the newness of life. (Romans 6:3-9)

Resurrection

ATMI believes in the bodily resurrection from the dead of the believer to everlasting joy with the Lord and of the unbeliever to judgment and everlasting conscious punishment. (Matthew 25, I Corinthians 15:35-58, II Corinthians 5:1-10, II Thessalonians 1:5-10.

The Church

ATMI believes that the Church is composed of all people who, through saving faith in Jesus Christ, are united together in the Body of Christ of which He is the head. (Ephesians 1:22, 2:14-22: 4:1-5)

ATMI believes that ordinances of the local church are believer's baptism and the Lords' Supper, Believers' baptism is a testimony of the death to sin resurrection to a new life in Christ and the Lord's Supper symbolizes the death of the Lord Jesus Christ and our salvation through faith in Him. All true believers should participate in these ordinances. (Matthew 26:26-29; 28:19-20, Acts 2:38-20, Romans 6:3-4, I Corinthians 11:17-32, Colossians 2:11-12)

Christ Return

ATMI believes that the personal and imminent return of our Lord Jesus Christ is our future hope and has a vital bearing on the personal life and service of the believer. (Matthew 24, John 14:1-4, I Thessalonians 4:16-18, Titus 2:11-14)

Spiritual Gifts of Christ to the Church

We believe in the development, activation, and service of the Five Fold ministry or Ascension gifts in the church, We believe that Jesus Christ gave gifts unto men and those gifts are to serve the body of Christ, for the maturing—perfection of the saints. (Ephesians 4:8-16, I Corinthians 12:1-4, Corinthians 14:1-5, I Corinthians 12:28)

Christian Responsibility

ATMI believes that the highest priorities for every believer are the great commandments: "Love the Lord your God with all your heart and with all your soul and all your mind . . . love your neighbor as yourself." These commands are fulfilled by glorifying God, enjoying Him, and fulfilling His great commission to go and make disciples of all nations. These pursuits require personal commitments to live by the truth of God's word and to depend on the power of His Spirit. Both the Word and the Spirit call us to a life of Christ-like character, wholehearted worship, generous giving, unselfish service, and compassionate outreach to the lost. (Matthew 22:37-40, Matthew 28:19-20, I Timothy 3:16, Ephesians 5:18-21, Ephesians 4:12-13, John 4:23-24, Luke 6:38, Matthew 20: 26-28, Luke 15)

Tithes & Offering & Alms Giving

ATMI **believes** that every believer should be a cheerful giver and sow into the ministry of the church. Every believer should have a true understanding of tithing, giving, and benevolence as the Word of God teaches. ATMI believes in the help and assistance to orphans, widows, and missions. (Heb 7:1-10, Matthew 10:38, Gen 14:17-20, Gen 28:22, Luke 6:38, Mark 10:29-30, II Corinthians 9:1, Philippians 4:17,

II Corinthians, 9:6-8, Malachi 3:8-12, Proverbs 3:9-10,)

Fulfilling Our Purpose In the Earth

In obedience to the Call of the Lord, Pastors John & Pamela Dillon (along with the ATMI team) heard the turbulence in the atmosphere to add to the Vision of Agape Time Ministries Inc.

We believe in our hearts that God has prepared us to build a pure place of worship where the Glory of the Lord may rest. The atmosphere will be set to usher the people of God into His presence 24 hours a day. Open to all that will hear the call to worship

This complex will be the central focal point for the coming together in unity of multi-cultural, multi-faceted ministries with the common goal of completing their individual as well as the corporate commission of the Body of Christ.

Our focus will be to stir up the gifts of the nation of end-time leaders/ potential leaders who have heard the call to operate in the spirit of excellence, integrity, accountability, and proper alignment, in ministry, and community affairs.

This complex will be open to all in the community to include Churches, Corporate entities, Political as well as Civic Leaders/ potential Leader.

We endeavor to forge a solid foundation for spiritual growth in the spirit of love, for the building of the Kingdom of God, with the emphasis on completing each assignment.

Our purpose is to sow seed of love to those in need of direction, and guidance for leadership. The ministry under the unction of the Holy Spirit well endeavor to preach and teach the uncompromising Word of God.

Our mandate is to provide a training facility, in an atmosphere conducive to managing, maintaining, and empowering the men and women of God with the necessary tools to impact their cities, states, and the nation. Whereby the Body of Christ will be motivated, strengthened, and equipped to walk in the ways **pleasing** to God both individually and corporately.

Our ATMI Staff is available to do:

Leadership Development
Training Workshops
Seminars
Conferences
Revivals
Retreats
Personal Counseling
Weddings
Prison Ministry
Youth Ministry

ATMI is a 501(c)3 not for profit organization

ADDITIONAL CLASSES AVAILABLE

<u>Week One:</u>

<u>The Spirit of an Armor—Bearer</u>

1. A heart of a Servant—Willing to Give their Life for the Life of others/Leader
2. *John 15:13: Greater love hath no man than this, that a man lay down his life for his friends*
3. Not seeking its own fame—able to walk in another vision-and help bring it to pass.
4. Trustworthy & Loyal—Privy to vital information not to be disclosed.
5. Dependable & faithful
6. Willing & Teachable & Submitted
7. Understanding—able to give grace and must have great respect for their leader.
8. Prayerful—add strength
9. Slow to Speak-Quiet Spirit—not argumentative.
10. Joyful
11. Not Cumbered with Life and It cares
12. The Spirit of an armor-bearer is the spirit of Christ
13. Humble & Lowly, meek
14. Powerful, persuasive,

<u>The Need for an Armor-Bearer</u>

1. To Lessen the Load of the Leader
2. To ASSIST IN carrying the Weight of the Assignment
3. To assist—with discretion
4. To come along side—Not ahead
5. To receive the impartation and training for their own assignment (Just because you train with them—does not mean you are ready to wear the armor.) Akeleis story.
6. To prepare a clear path
7. To protect

<u>Definition of the Word Armor-bearer</u>

Two Hebrew Word =Nasa or Nacah pronounced—(Naw-Saw)—To lift accept, advance, bear up carry away, cast, desire, furnish give help pardon raise, regard, respect. Stir up, yield.

2nd word= kel-ee comes from the root word Kalah pronounced (kaw-law)—to end or complete, consume, destroy utterly, be done, finish, fulfill. Long, bring to pass wholly reap, make clean

Literally to stand beside his/her leader to assist them, to lift them up and to protect them against any enemy that might attack them.

Week Two:

The Functions & Role of the Armor—Bearer

1. Must provide strength for his leader—Leader cannot be concerned or have to carry the weight of the armor-bearer. Many times leaders are drained physically and emotionally from carry the weight and concerns of armor bearer and members/other leaders.
2. Must have a deep-down sense of respect for his Leader, acceptance, tolerance, & grace.
3. Must instinctively understand their Leader's thoughts.
4. Must walk in agreement with and healthy submission to their leader.
5. Must make the advancement of his leader his most important goal
6. Must possess endless strength so as to thrust, press and force his way onward without giving way under harsh treatment I Peter 2:20—there are times in the midst of serving in battle that you will feel mistreated. Do not allow Satan to put resentment in your heart.
7. Must follow orders immediately and correctly.
8. Must be a support to his leader
9. Must be an excellent communicator
10. Must have a disposition that will eagerly gain victories for his leader.
11. Must have the ability to minister strength and courage to their leader.
12. Must be able to launch and adjust quickly.
13. Must be a team player

In addition to this teaching we offer a Power Point Slide Show of Intense Armor-Bearer Training. This particular training is for those call to walk alongside closely with their leaders in a different realm of covenant. This series is called. "Armor Bearer Training-Serving from the Heart of God" and "I Carry more than the Armor".

Note: These are the Teacher/Speaker Note—Not a Hand Out.

Monday Night Teaching-

Brazen Altar Teachings

    📖   Revelation: Getting Closer to God—Should not become a ritual or made an idol—But a surrender and submission.

July 18th—2011—2nd Session—2nd teaching—Every time we shun evil we bring God's Glory into the earth.

My Prayer Becomes My offering . . .

    📖   Romans 12:1 . . . Present your Bodies a Living sacrifice Holy & Acceptable
    📖   Leviticus 1:4-9
    📖   Psalms 51: 3 Acknowledge my sin.

Acts 3:19 . . . Repent, therefore and be converted that your sins may be blotted out, so that that times of refreshing may come from the presence of the Lord—a submission

    ➤   Korbanos: An offering which means drawing closer to God
    ➤   **Chatat: Sin Offerings**
    ➤   A sin offering is an offering to atone for and purge a sin. It is an expression of sorrow for the error and a desire to be reconciled with <u>G-d</u>. The Hebrew term for this type of offering is chatat, from the word chayt, meaning "missing the mark." A chatat could only be offered for unintentional sins committed through carelessness, not for intentional, malicious sins. The size of the offering varied according to the nature of the sin and the financial means of the sinner. Some chatatot are individual and some are communal. Communal offerings represent the interdependence of the community, and the fact that we are all responsible for each others' sins. A few special chatatot could not be eaten, but for the most part, for the average person's personal sin, the chatat was eaten by the <u>kohanim</u>. (Note this portion of Chatat taken from a internet website author known)
    ➤   Teshuvah: Hebrew word which means return . . . It means we return to the path God set for us when we were born, the path that our souls know as homeward bound, the path of goodness, of becoming a better person.

Brazen Altar Teaching I must become a sacrifice before I can become an offering.

The process of killing the sacrifice.

- ❖ The Believer brought the offering to the door
- ❖ Sacrifice killed at the door.
- ❖ Why now that I am save so many things are going wrong . . . I enter the gate with thanksgiving and into his courts with praise.
- ❖ I have to acknowledge and go through something experience sufferings
- ❖ I can't regret the process. I must find a need and honor and a benefit of going through and completing the process.
- ❖ I cannot view the process of death and dying to myself as some evil/mean occurrence or a bad happening God is doing 2 me.
- ❖ Each of us is subject to his own temptations some to money, lust, glory and power. Whatever our spiritual station, When Adam was created his nature was to do good. He was not the mixture of good and evil inclinations that human beings have today. Adams' innate nature was good and to perform nothing but the will of His maker. The Key: Adam was created with a Freewill.
- ❖ Evil presented from the outside the temple. Now—man's struggle is from within-
- ❖ After the fall of Man we resound to sin not from outside force but our own desires
- ❖ Since Adam is so pure what made him swayed by outside temptation.
- ❖ Adams mission was to elevate himself where he pleased God all the time.
- ❖ He was deceived into thinking that this knowledge would make him closer to God
- ❖ Adam should have persevered himself during the few hours between his creation and the onset of the first Sabbath. He did not enter into the place of rest.
- ❖ Purpose of creation to bring God Glory into the earth.

July 25, 2011—Brazen Altar

Topic: I must become a sacrifice before I can become an offering.

- • Romans 12: Leviticus 1: 4-9 Psalm 51:17-17 The sacrifices of God are a broken spirit: and a contrite heart.
- • Becoming a sacrifice.
  1. Acknowledging—verbally confessing that I have something to bring
  2. Sacrifice giving up something that is of valuable and appears irreplaceable
  3. Something I have gained through working for it or praying for it.
  4. Sacrifice requires an action you can't justify
  5. Sacrifice requires an act you don't understand not logical
  6. In the sacrifice there is a struggle—Abraham and Isaac
  7. Putting something to death that you desire
  8. Something you feel you truly need or can't live without
  9. The sacrifice must be voluntary. Voluntary will . . .

10. You don't want a hostel take over.
   - ❖ Why a male sacrifice . . . What does it represent . . .
   - ❖ Male: Authority—Strength . . . Human strength
   - ❖ You must sacrifice your authority and control over a matter.
   - ❖ Sacrifice must be killed in the presence of the Lord . . . a sweet surrender
   - ❖ If killed on your own=sustaining=resentment and rebellion . . . self fulfillment.
   - ❖ Offering the exchange or transfer.

God is not really interested in my possessions—He is interested in my heart.

Do Not be caught up in the technical and regulations of the offerings but the spiritual

Aug 1, 2011

- ❖ Sacrifice must be killed in the presence of the Lord . . . a sweet surrender
- ❖ If killed on your own=sustaining=resentment and rebellion . . . self fulfillment.
- ❖ In the sacrifice there is a struggle—Abraham and Isaac

Prayer of . . . A service of the Heart.

God has no need for the animal sacrifice anymore. God is after my heart which in turn causes me to surrender my life.

Jesus Christ became the Ultimate Sacrifice. He overcame death and conquered the grave. No need for me to physically die to live a sacrificial life.

Aug 1, 2011—Brazen Altar Teaching

New International Version (NIV)

- 📖 **Romans 6:4**
- 📖 We were therefore **buried with** him through baptism into death in order that, just as **Christ** was raised from the dead through the glory of the Father, we too may live a new life.

- 📖 **Ecclesiastes 5:19**
- 📖 Moreover, when **God** gives someone wealth and possessions, and the ability to enjoy them, to accept their lot and be happy in their toil—this is a **gift of God**.

📖 **Deuteronomy 12:11**

📖 Then to the place the LORD your **God** will choose as a dwelling for his Name—there you are to bring everything I command you: your burnt **offerings** and sacrifices, your tithes and special **gifts**, and all the choice possessions you have vowed to the LORD.

📖 Deuteronomy 12:10-12 (in Context) Deuteronomy 12 (Whole Chapter)

📖 **Leviticus 9:24**

📖 Fire came out from the presence of the LORD and consumed the **burnt offering** and the fat portions on the altar. And when all the people saw it, they shouted for joy and fell facedown.

📖 Leviticus 9:23-24 (in Context) Leviticus 9 (Whole Chapter)

📖 **Leviticus 9:13**

📖 They handed him the **burnt offering** piece by piece, including the head, and he burned them on the altar.

📖 **Leviticus 9:16**

📖 He brought the **burnt offering** and offered it in the prescribed way.

📖 Leviticus 9:15-17 (in Context) Leviticus 9 (Whole Chapter)

The Brazen Altar was the largest piece of furniture in the Tabernacle, 7ft. 6ins. long, 7ft. 6in. in width and 4ft. 6in. high, overlaid with brass on shittim or acacia wood. Smoke ascending from the sacrifice may have been a figure of the offering rising to fellowship with God, while Peter wrote, "Christ also hath once suffered for sins, the just for the unjust, that he might bring us to God . . ." (1 Pet. 3:18).

- My heart is where my will and emotions are located
- My heart is the seat of human emotion, affections, desire, passion, love and all other feelings.
- The heart is the center of true thoughts, ideas, and desires
- The heart dictates our behavior—conduct—attitude

📖 **Matthew 6:19**

📖 [*Treasures in Heaven*] "Do not store up for yourselves **treasures** on earth, where moths and vermin destroy, and where thieves break in and steal.

📖 Matthew 6:18-20 (in Context) Matthew 6 (Whole Chapter)

    📖   <u>Matthew 6:20</u>

    📖   But store up for yourselves **treasures** in heaven, where moths and vermin do not destroy, and where thieves do not break in and steal.

    📖   <u>Matthew 6:19-21</u> (in Context) <u>Matthew 6</u> (Whole Chapter)

Proverbs 24:4

King James Version (KJV)

[4]And by knowledge shall the chambers be filled with all precious and pleasant riches.

1. <u>1 Chronicles 29:3</u>
2. Besides, in my devotion to the temple of my God I now give my personal **treasures** of gold and silver for the temple of my God, over and above everything I have provided for this holy temple:
3. <u>1 Chronicles 29:2-4</u> (in Context) <u>1 Chronicles 29</u> (Whole Chapter)

<u>Hebrews 10:19-22</u>—Therefore, brothers, since we have confidence to enter the Most Holy Place by the blood of Jesus, by a new and living way opened for us through the curtain, that is, His body, and since we have a great Priest over the house of God, let us draw near to God with a sincere heart in full assurance of faith, having our hearts sprinkled to cleanse us from a guilty conscience and having our bodies washed with pure water.

101. <u>1 Chronicles 22:19</u>
102. Now devote your heart and soul to seeking the LORD your God. Begin to build the sanctuary of the LORD God, so that you may bring the ark of the covenant of the LORD and the sacred articles belonging to God into the temple that will be built for the Name of the LORD."
103. <u>1 Chronicles 22:18-19</u> (in Context) <u>1 Chronicles 22</u> (Whole Chapter)

My reason for Dying is to Live Again. Jesus was buried and than Resurrected.

<u>August 29, 2011</u>

Replacement Value<u>. . . Making An Exchange of Unholy things for Holy Things</u>

Dying to One's Self brings the Glory to the temple.

Jesus was buried in a tomb . . . 3 days . . . Sealed Shut Doors . . . Standing Guard . . .

📖 ¹ The LORD said to Moses, ² "Tell the Israelites to bring me an offering. You are to receive the offering for me from everyone whose heart prompts them to give. ³ These are the offerings you are to receive from them: gold, silver and bronze; ⁴ blue, purple and scarlet yarn and fine linen; goat hair; ⁵ ram skins dyed red and another type of durable leather[a]; acacia wood; ⁶ olive oil for the light; spices for the anointing oil and for the fragrant incense; ⁷ and onyx stones and other gems to be mounted on the ephod and breast piece.

⁸ "Then have them make a sanctuary for me, and I will dwell among them.

Galatians 2:19-20 New International Version (NIV)

¹⁹ "For through the law I died to the law so that I might live for God. ²⁰ I have been crucified with Christ and I no longer live, but Christ lives in me. The life I now live in the body, I live by faith in the Son of God, who loved me and gave himself for me.

📖 **Galatians 5:18-23**
📖 <u>¹⁸ **But if you are led by the Spirit, you are not under the law.**</u>
📖 ¹⁹ The acts of the flesh are obvious: sexual immorality, impurity and debauchery; ²⁰ idolatry and witchcraft; hatred, discord, jealousy, fits of rage, selfish ambition, dissensions, factions
📖 ²¹ and envy; drunkenness, orgies, and the like. I warn you, as I did before, that those who live like this will not inherit the kingdom of God.
📖 ²² But the fruit of the Spirit is love, joy, peace, forbearance, kindness, goodness, faithfulness, ²³ gentleness and self-control. Against such things there is no law.
  • Jesus replaced: Death—Life
  • Hate for Love
  • Lack for abundance
  • Fear for confidence—Power of love
  • Confusion . . . sound mind

Preceding Forward into the Holy Place.—Sacrifice to Offering. Living offering to Sanctuary

1. Word cannot be received without the Fruit of the Spirit.
2. love, joy, peace, forbearance, kindness, goodness, faithfulness, ²³ gentleness and self-control. Against such things there is no law.

<u>**How Do I kill the Flesh:**</u> I exchange it for the Fruit of the Spirit.

<u>Issues or Hindrances to becoming the sacrifice</u>

1. 1st a Sacrifice before I can become an offering. I make my mind up at the gate.
2. AT the door is where the decision was made . . . Leviticus 1:3-5 Voluntary will at the door the sacrifice was killed. And place on the Altar as an offering.
3. Battling with the process of the death I a not making the exchange
   The Struggle is not in giving it up. It is in the memory of having it and the emotions one experiences. The law that has been set up in my members.
4. There is a law established in my flesh since the fall that I want to keep.
5. I must assassinate the Law of the flesh with the Spirit of God.

<u>Make the Exchange</u>

- Exchange animalistic behavior for the behavior the Fruit of The Spirit.
- The Behavior of the Holy One.
- I must replace the burnt offering the sacrifice with the fruit
- I must fill the void.
- Jesus replaces the law of your sinful nature . . .
- A gift is transforming.
- A gift contains God's presence.
- Gods' presence . . . His essence is the manifestation and the epitome of the fruit.

I am Refined by the Fire . . .

<u>September 12, 2011-</u>

Related By the Blood . . . What's Up With the Blood?

DNA: I have the authority the power,—the resurrection—dying stamina from the Blood of Jesus Christ.

The Life is in the Blood . . . The Life of the Flesh is in the Blood . . .

Scriptures:

"He is to lay his hand on the head of the burnt offering, and it will be accepted on his behalf to make atonement for him." (Leviticus 1:4)

"For the life of a creature is in the blood, and I have given it to you to make atonement for yourselves on the altar; it is the blood that makes atonement for one's life." (Leviticus 17:11)

"The law requires that nearly everything be cleansed with blood, and without the shedding of blood there is no forgiveness." (Hebrews 9:22)

"This is my blood of the covenant, which is poured out for many." (Mark 14:24)

"For you know that . . . you were redeemed . . . with the precious blood of Christ, a lamb without blemish or defect." (1 Peter 1:18-19)

"The blood of goats and bulls and the ashes of a heifer sprinkled on those who are ceremonially unclean sanctify them so that they are outwardly clean. How much more, then, will the blood of Christ, who through the eternal Spirit offered himself unblemished to God, cleanse our consciences from acts that lead to death, so that we may serve the living God!" (Hebrews 9:13-14)

"We have been made holy through the sacrifice of the body of Jesus Christ once for all . . . By one sacrifice he has made perfect forever those who are being made holy . . . And where these have been forgiven, there is no longer any sacrifice for sin." (Hebrews 10:10, 14, 18)

God made him who had no sin to be sin for us, so that in him we might become the righteousness of God." (2 Corinthians 5:21)

1. Horns were a symbol power and strength in biblical times. When the sacrifice was made, blood was dabbed on the horns of the altar, signifying the power of the blood to atone for sins. In the same way, there is mighty power in the blood of Christ. Jesus is the "horn of our salvation" (Psalm 18:2, Luke 1:69).
    *   By laying his hand upon the head of the offering, the person was identifying with the sacrifice. His sin and guilt was being moved from himself to the animal. 2.
    *   The priest would then slaughter the animal, sprinkle its blood in front of the <u>veil</u> of the Holy Place, burn the sacrifice, and pour the rest of it at the bottom of the altar. 3.
    *   Blood is a significant agent of <u>atonement</u> (covering for sin; click on link to read more detailed definition) and cleansing in the Old Testament.
    *   **Atonement=covering of Sin. Blood was the agent.**

Strength through the Blood.—The Horns of the Altar

The Significance of the Tabernacle Sacrifices

1. Although the blood of the sacrifices covered over the sins of the Israelites, they had to perform the sacrifices year after year, for they were not freed permanently of a guilty conscience.

2. However, Jesus Christ, the Lamb of God, came as the ultimate and last sacrifice for mankind when He offered up His life. As Isaiah prophesied, the Christ would be like a lamb that is led to slaughter <u>and</u> pierced for our transgressions. His blood was sprinkled and poured out at the cross for us. The Bible says much about this:
    1. **Everything about me needs to been cleanses by the blood**
    2. **Agent: The Blood covering caused me to be a legal agent for Christ.**

<u>Agent:</u>

1. a person or business authorized to act on another's behalf: *Our agent in Hong Kong will ship the merchandise. A best-selling author needs a good agent.*
2. a person or thing that acts or has the power to act.
3. a natural force or object producing or used for obtaining specific results: *Many insects are agents of fertilization.*
4. an active cause; an efficient cause.
5. a person who works for or manages an <u>agency</u>.
    3. **No longer animalistic behavior—but the Godly behavior**
    4. **Blood transfusion—For Blood transformation**

3. A blood transfusion is a safe, common procedure in which blood is given to you through an intravenous (IV) line in one of your blood vessels.

4. Blood transfusions are done to replace blood lost during surgery or due to a serious injury. A transfusion also may be done if your body can't make blood properly because of an illness.

<u>Covenant:</u> an agreement, usually formal, between two or more persons to do or not do something specified. the conditional promises made to humanity by God, as revealed in Scripture. the agreement between God and the ancient Israelites, in which God promised to protect them if they kept His law and were faithful to Him.

The animal sacrifices bore reference to the Passover lambs, which the Israelites slaughtered in like manner to save their firstborns from the last plague of God's judgment on Egypt (Exodus 12:1-13). Similarly, as the Passover lambs were eaten after they were slaughtered, some of the sacrificial lambs also were eaten. Just as the sacrificial lambs were **sacrificed and eaten**, so Jesus' body was **sacrificed and "eaten."** It was no coincidence that on the night before the Passover when Jesus was crucified, He "took bread, gave thanks and broke it, and gave it to his disciples, saying, 'Take and eat; this is my body'" (Matthew 26:26). Earlier Jesus had taught His disciples:

Oct 3, 2011

Scriptures Leviticus 20:7-8 New International Version (NIV)

7 "'Consecrate yourselves and be holy, because I am the LORD your God. 8 Keep my decrees and follow them. I am the LORD, who makes you holy.

    📖 Exodus 30:18

    📖 "You shall also make a **laver** of bronze, with its base also of bronze, for washing. You shall put it between the tabernacle of meeting and the altar. And you shall put water in it,)

    📖 Exodus 38:8

    📖 [*Making the Bronze Laver*] He made the **laver** of bronze and its base of bronze, from the bronze mirrors of the serving women who assembled at the door of the tabernacle of meeting.

    📖 James 1:23-24
    📖 New International Version (NIV)
    📖 23 Anyone who listens to the word but does not do what it says is like someone who looks at his face in a mirror 24 and, after looking at himself, goes away and immediately forgets what he looks like.

    📖 1 Corinthians 3:16-17
    📖 New International Version (NIV)
    📖 16 Don't you know that you yourselves are God's temple and that God's Spirit dwells in your midst? 17 If anyone destroys God's temple, God will destroy that person; for God's temple is sacred, and you together are that temple.

II Corinthians 6:162 Corinthians 6:16-17

New International Version (NIV)

16 What agreement is there between the temple of God and idols? For we are the temple of the living God. As God has said:

"I will live with them and walk among them, and I will be their God,   and they will be my people."[a] 17 Therefore,   "Come out from them   and be separate, says the Lord. Touch no unclean thing,

<u>Ephesians 5:26</u>

to make her holy, cleansing her by the **washing** with water through the word,

<u>Oct 3, 2011</u>—

Brazen Laver—Kiyyor—Hebrew—means port, pan laver Basin . . . Bowl—Outer Court

- ➤ Time to Clean Up . . .
- ➤ It Offering Time . . .
- ➤ God is preparing me right now to be an offering to his people.

I must become a sacrifice before an offering. Sacrifice on the Altar—Now to becoming an offering. Yom Kippur the High Priest—Cohen Gadol—with thru a personal cleansing before, going on the behalf of the people.

The Lord's desire is for me to be sanctified—set apart. Adonai M'Kaddesh-The Lord who sanctifies . . . To make whole set apart for holiness.

Bronze or Brazen . . .

1. Made of Bronze or Brazen . . . meaning man

2. Made from the mirrors and looking glasses of the women—The women used the mirrors prior to beautify themselves for their husbands.
   - The Mirror Has a twofold task or operation.
   - It causes two reflections.
   - My will and what I presently look like.
   - God's will and what I can become. The Mirror gives a view of what you can become through Christ.
   - The word manifested in me brings about the reflection and image of Christ.
   - The washing reveals the residue . . . any defilements . . . or fat . . . letf.
   - I must scrub or wash off
   - He saved us through the washing of rebirth and renewal by the Holy Spirit,- Titus 3:5
   - The Flaws and the Beauty will be revealed.
   - I must simultaneously see the sin, the shame, and the overcomer.
   - The Blood must be applied.
   - What washes away my sin The Blood of Jesus Christ.
   - Water—Represents the Holy Spirit.

What Had to be Washed.—Before I dressed for Service

- The priest had to wash in laver before enter the Inner Court
- Wash feet—my walk in God my destiny—my journey
  My hands—for service—touching—transferring, and impartation
- The Brazen or Bronze laver was for the Priest not for God.
- The word Priest in Hebrew is—Cohen-before there were Catholic or Episcopal priests there were Jewish priests.—The Cohanim
- Before the Jewish priest there was another priest o f somewhat a mysterious origin . . . His name is Melchizedek meaning king of righteousness and he appeared 422 years before the law was given.
- Genesis 14: 17-18 Melchizedek was both a king and a priest. He was called the priest of the most High God
- Melchizedek was without father and mother—this indicated that he was a priest who did not inherit the priesthood from his parents. He did not come from a priestly line.
- This hope we have as an anchor of the soul, both sure and steadfast, and which enters the Presence behind the veil, where the forerunner has entered for us, even Yeshua, having become High Priest forever according to the order of Malki-Tzedek (Hebrew 6:19-20)

Oct 10, 2011—

3. Priest—Intercessors I Peter 2:9) royal priesthood.
4. Undressing and Re dressing. The Cohen Gadol of the Torah and the Levicitical Priests our Great High Priest. They were a shadow of the good things to come.—A type, a picture of a future reality—a perfect High Priest—the Son of God—Yeshua—Jesus the Christ.

Menorah Teachings

April 30, 2012   **Hammered Out**

Scriptures: Exodus 25:31—King James Version (KJV)

Hammering and Beaten

[31]And thou shalt make a candlestick of pure gold: of beaten work shall the candlestick be made: his shaft, and his branches, his bowls, his knops, and his flowers, shall be of the same.

Exodus 25:31—New King James Version (NKJV) The Gold Lampstand

[31] "You shall also make a lampstand of pure gold; the lampstand shall be of hammered work. Its shaft, its branches, its bowls, its *ornamental* knobs, and flowers shall be *of one piece.*

Endurance

1 Corinthians 13:7

Beareth all things, believeth all things, hopeth all things, **endureth** all things.

1. **James 1:12**
2. Blessed is the man that **endureth** temptation: for when he is tried, he shall receive the crown of life, which the Lord hath promised to them that love him.
3. Whole Chapter)

Suffering

4. **Romans 8:18**
5. For I reckon that the **sufferings** of this present time are not worthy to be compared with the glory which shall be revealed in us.
6. **2 Corinthians 1:5**
7. For as the **suffering**s of Christ abound in us, so our consolation also aboundeth by Christ.
8. **2 Corinthians 1:6**
9. And whether we be afflicted, it is for your consolation and salvation, which is effectual in the enduring of the same **sufferings** which we also suffer: or whether we be comforted, it is for your consolation and salvation.
10. **2 Corinthians 1:7**
11. And our hope of you is stedfast, knowing, that as ye are partakers of the **sufferings**, so shall ye be also of the consolation.
12. **2 Corinthians 6:6**
13. By pureness, by knowledge, by long **suffering**, by kindness, by the Holy Ghost, by love unfeigned,
14. **Philippians 3:10**
15. That I may know him, and the power of his resurrection, and the fellowship of his **suffering**s, being made conformable unto his death;
16. Philippians 3:9-11 (in Context) Philippians 3 (Whole Chapter)

Definitions:

Revelation: **Continuous force or pressure to a certain area until the desired shape has been achieved.**

<u>Hammer:</u> to strike blows especially repeatedly with or as if with a hammer: POUND: to make repeated efforts; *especially*: to reiterate an opinion or attitude (hammered away at same points>

a: to beat, drive, or shape with repeated blows of a hammer *b*: to fasten or build with a hammer
: to strike or drive with a force suggesting a hammer blow or repeated blows <*hammered* the ball over the fence> <tried to *hammer* me into submission>

Positive Part of Hammer:

A Beaten Work:

<u>Beat:</u> to progress with much difficulty: *a*: OVERCOME, DEFEAT; *also*: SURPASS—often used with *out*: to strike repeatedly: *a*: to hit repeatedly so as to inflict pain—often used with *up b*: to walk on: TREAD <*beat* the pavement looking for work> *c*: or as if in quest of game *f*: to mix by stirring: WHIP with *up g*: to strike repeatedly in order to produce music or a signal <*beat* a drum>

The Menorah Made from one piece of Gold:

1. When Gold is extracted from the earth it has no value until it goes through purification process
2. You must go through a purification process before you can be used by G-d—A worthy vessel

In The Purifying Process:

- ➤ Impurities are removed
- ➤ In the fire is where the gold is made and manifest
- ➤ After gold is melted down and withstood the process. Now ready to be fashioned by the goldsmith
- ➤ G-d the Goldsmith—In his hands you are made.

<u>What Does the Hammering Look like?</u>

- ➢ Hammering Hurts—It is Painful
- ➢ Life Events-Relationships—Financial set backs—
- ➢ Trials—Testing-Suffering
- ➢ Revelation: Suffering: When You have did nothing to deserve—what is happening to you.
- ➢ The hammering-is not warranted. It is just for the making.
- ➢ All for G-d divine purpose to make you a beaten vessel. A Menorah to the World.
- ➢ Levels of Process: Yield through the Process
- ➢ Quick process submit to the process—You determine the length of beating.
- ➢ Make the Music As-you are hammered you ask questions—Log your learning— Log your pain-

Menorah Teaching

April 16, 2012—

Natural Light—Artificial Light—Holy Light-Which Light Do you Operate?

- ➢ Scriptures:

<u>Exodus; 25:37</u> And thou shalt make the lamps thereof, seven; and they shall light the lamps thereof, to give light over against it.

- ➢ **<u>Zechariah 4:1-6 New International Version (NIV)</u>**

Zechariah 4—The Gold Lampstand and the Two Olive Trees

[1] Then the angel who talked with me returned and woke me up, like someone awakened from sleep. [2] He asked me, "What do you see?"

I answered, "I see a solid gold lampstand with a bowl at the top and seven lamps on it, with seven channels to the lamps. [3] Also there are two olive trees by it, one on the right of the bowl and the other on its left."

[4] I asked the angel who talked with me, "What are these, my lord?"

[5] He answered, "Do you not know what these are?"

"No, my lord," I replied.

[6] So he said to me, "This is the word of the LORD to Zerubbabel: 'Not by might nor by power, but by my Spirit,' says the LORD Almighty.

- ➤ **Psalm 104:4**
- ➤ He makes winds his messengers, **flames of fire** his servants.
- ➤ **1 Corinthians 15:46**
- ➤ The spiritual did not come first, but the **natural**, and after that the spiritual.

Types of Light:

Natural Light= Natural understanding born with . . . Natural love and natural joy. Vigor for life.

a: occurring in conformity with the ordinary course of nature: not marvelous or supernatural <*natural* causes> *b*: formulated by human reason alone rather than revelation <*natural* religion> <*natural* rights> *c*: having a normal or usual character <events followed their *natural* course>

a: being in a state of nature without spiritual enlightenment: UNREGENERATE <*natural* man>

Artificial Light= Not your true nature—or true natural . . . mock light—Not the real light . . . knowledge I have attained from observing or reading. Something I have gained knowledge in with no inner understanding.

obsolete: ARTFUL, CUNNING 4*a*: lacking in natural or spontaneous quality <an *artificial* smile> <an *artificial* excitement> *b*: IMITATION, SHAM <*artificial* flavor>

5: based on differential morphological characters not necessarily indicative of natural relationships <an *artificial* key for plant identification>

Holy Light=Menorah Light= My Natural light marries the light of G-d. G-d's light connects with my light to make super natural light . . . = Revelation . . .

spiritual illumination *b*: INNER LIGHT *c*: ENLIGHTENMENT *d*: TRUTH something that makes vision possible *b*: the sensation aroused by stimulation of the visual receptors *c*: electromagnetic radiation of any <u>wavelength that travels in a vacuum with a speed of about 186,281 miles (300,000 kilometers) per second;</u> *specifically*: such radiation that is visible to the human eye

2*a*: DAYLIGHT *b*: DAWN 3: a source of light: as *a*: a celestial body

Revelation= G-dly wisdom and understanding. Revealed knowledge from eternity.

Oil from life—Oil from me—gives me experience—mixed with my faith from G-d causes me to light the Menorah light.

Pure Flames: What Color is Your Personal Flame?

- The Hottest flame is not Red, Orange, Yellow, or Blue
- White is The Purest Flame:—The Purest Anointing—Revelation.

The Priest: The *kohanim* lit the menorah in the Sanctuary every evening and cleaned it out every morning, replacing the replacing the wicks and putting fresh olive oil into the cups.

S.W.A.T TEAM
TESTIMONIES

We would be remiss to not include testimonials of those who have partaken of Agape Time Ministries-City of Refuge—Training Facility . . . Please take the opportunity to read these life changing real stories.

Jaron Simon

When I arrived back home to Saint Louis on December 28, 2010, I felt an overwhelming burden to begin the process of looking for a new church home. I was a recent college graduate, not even two weeks out of school, and I had spent the last five years in Columbia, Missouri (where I attended college at the University of Missouri) going from church to church. I was a nomad. I found no church that provided all of what I was looking for. There are no "perfect churches" but I knew in the depths of my soul that I was not fulfilled.

There was a church in Saint Louis that I had in mind to join, and although I loved the pastors and the church, for whatever reason I never became settled with becoming a member there. In the midst of being weighed down

with the burden of visiting new churches, the Lord's providence intervened. I crossed paths with Brandon Fulks, a long time friend who I had not seen in years, on January 1, 2011 at a New Year's Day Concert. It was in reuniting that I learned that Brandon was a member of Agape Time Ministries and he invited me to visit on January 4th to see him teach a Tuesday night class. I accepted his invitation and he taught powerfully on the topic of commitment. After class, Pastors John and Pamela Dillon (the pastors of Agape Time) gave encouraging words to Brandon concerning the teaching, and the entire class went around giving accolades.

That first night at Agape Time was a transition marked with highs and lows. It was low because that same morning my relationship of almost two years came to an end and I became single. Yet, it was high because there was no denying that I was on to something. There was something real at Agape Time. I remember Pastor John exhibiting a trait that I had long desired to have in a pastor and that is proximity. I have attended different churches where the biblical word was preached, yet I could not touch the pastors. There was no discipleship and that is what my soul longed for. I desired a man of God to pour into me and show me the way to maturity. What I sought out was a spiritual father (much like 1 Corinthians 4:15). Pastor John, in one of the most down to earth manners, came over and began to converse with me. I could not figure out why, but I felt safe talking to him. I could trust him. I told him of the heartbreak of becoming single and of the uncertainty of discovering the next steps in life. He began to pour into me and speak encouraging words that were hardly generic. They were specific words; words that were full of wisdom and the Spirit of God.

The moment that sealed it for me was when he spoke exactly of that which I was in pursuit of. Not even an hour into our conversation he said, "See, what you are really in search of is a spiritual father; someone who can walk with you and alongside you into maturity. When you discover this man of God, you will know who he is and he will know who you are as his spiritual son." Quite astonished, I thought to myself, "How is that I have known this man for only a moment yet he knows exactly what I stand in need of!?" After our empowering conversation, Pastor Pam also came in and they both prayed for me. I knew that I had found something real. But, because it happened so effortlessly and suddenly my logic would not allow me to be at peace. I thought to myself, "Lord, I was just talking to you about the burden of having to find a church home, of taking my time in searching, and this has come already?" I could not believe it but I also could not shake it. I prayed and battled with my logic for about two weeks and then finally submitted to the peace that I had concerning Agape Time.

Since joining the ministry, I have enjoyed gut wrenching laughter, suffered affliction, engaged in spiritual warfare, and developed camaraderie. I have enjoyed fellowship in a community that can be likened to the church in Acts and I have been equipped in a way that is outlined in Ephesians 4:11-12. My time has been full of difficulty that has been coupled with the joy of the Lord as my strength. It has been filled with death to self that has been coupled with the grace of Jesus to endure and die thousands of times daily (as Pastor Pam teaches). Most importantly, it has been full of encounters with the Lord that have birthed in me a greater love and gratitude for Him. I thank God for sending me a spiritual father and mother in Pastor John and Pastor Pam. I thank God for their transparency; for their willingness to share their life's tribulations and to reveal their imperfections. They are a selfless unit who have not only counseled, discipled, and encouraged me through life, but have taught me to seek the face of God more passionately! With maturity (and humility), I have learned that there is certainly a place to receive encouragement in the Lord from others, but as a mature believer, it is no longer acceptable to depend entirely on the word of God given through the mouths and writings of others when I have access to the very same God. I must dine at the Lord's Table for myself. I press on learning to walk in greater maturity, to wait on the Lord, to be confident in the Lord, and to trust in His guidance. My soul has found rest in the Lord at Agape Time and I am honored to call it my church home.

Jaron T. Simon (pronounced like 'Aaron')
Wednesday, January 11, 2012

Mother and Son, Curtis & Pamela Wilson

With lovingkindness have I drawn thee.
Jeremiah 31:3b.

I met my pastors, John and Pamela Dillon, at a time of brokenness in my life. Just a few days later, they took the time to sit down and talk—*really talk*—with me. Not as a matter of formality or procedure, but as people who took a genuine interest in me and demonstrated a sincere concern not just with the turmoil that was going on in my present, but with how God's perfect plan was taking me to my future. They were committed and remain committed to ushering me into God's divine purpose for my life.

Tell Archippus: "See to it that you complete the work you have received in the Lord."
Colossians 4:17

I have said before and will say now, that had God not caused me to cross paths with my pastors, I very likely would have aborted a major purpose He has for my life.

After being at ATMI for only a couple of weeks, I reluctantly asked Pastor Pam if she would care to see some of my writings. I say reluctantly because, although I have been writing for as long as I can remember and had already published two books, my confidence that what I had to offer this time was shaky at best. That was because these current writings were much different and had already been rejected by the traditional church. Pastor Pam was not only willing, but genuinely excited to read my work. Despite her incredibly busy schedule she made time to read each one and to give me immediate feedback and encouragement. Both Pastor Pam and Pastor John helped me to understand that what God was giving me to write would likely never be accepted by most traditional churches—that it was for a new generation and that in this "new" generation, chronological age is really of no consequence. Those of the "new" generation are open to what God is saying to His people and however He chooses to say it for this day and time.

Be thou diligent to know the state of thy flocks, *and* **look well to thy herds.**

Proverbs 27:23

As evidence of the above-mentioned "new" generation having no relationship to chronological age, unlike most of the members of ATMI, I am over forty. Okay . . . actually way over. The mentorship and relationship Pastors Dillon extend to all of the people God has entrusted to them, to me, is the key integral component of what makes them as pastors and ATMI as a ministry vastly different from what one finds in most church experiences and I, for one, will remain eternally grateful.

Monique Renee Fulks

When I came to Agape Time Ministries, I was a broken young lady in search for something that seemed to be intangible. I had been badly hurt by family, friends, church members and even Christian leadership. I was on a quest to find something greater and more fulfilling than what I was accustomed to. I wanted more of G-d and I knew that my spirit, my mind, and even my health were in dying states. I was invited by Pastor Pam, through my fiancée, to come to the grand opening and be the guest psalmist for the evening.

As I sat and observed the atmosphere, and I really felt the peace of The Lord in the place. I felt as if I were home and safe from all of the outside world that would try to harm me. I was currently a member of another ministry, but I asked the lord, "can I leave Lord? I want to be here." At that moment, Pastor John turned to me and said, "I heard you. You can come on. We will take care of you."

I was completely shocked! How did he hear me? I prayed that prayer to myself . . . he knows The Lord for real! So, I started coming to the weekly services they had to offer, and quickly joined the ministry with G-ds permission. I began to grow and fill the void that had been with me for so long being filled. I began to feel whole and really understand who I am in Christ and the giftings that He has placed on the inside me. I have been a part of the ministry for over a year now and I love G-d more than I ever have before. I am currently over the worship ministry, a part of the children's teaching staff, am involved as a teacher for Tuesday night class, and I love every moment of everything that I'm doing. I am walking into my callings of evangelism and many other things. Now, I am the happiest that I have been in years. I hear the lord quicker and more clearly and the only thing I'm searching for is more of Christ! I thank G-d for Agape Time Ministries.

Monique Renee

Tracy Jackson

Tracy Jackson's Journey to Agape Time Ministries

I have always been a little different from my friends no matter how hard I have tried to force myself to fit in. I was that little triangle that was trying to be that square. I've always dreamt vivid and detailed dreams and see things that "weren't there". I wasn't until 7 years old I started asking questions. I mean who dreams about the exact location where her mother has misplaced something? Yeah . . . I was that girl. No one could fully answer all the questions that I had pertaining to these things—although my mom did the best she knew how to do. I always felt that there was so much more. So I stopped asking questions and just started writing the things that I saw, heard, felt and even smelled on some occasions.

I am an identical twin and we have always had the ability to pull people to us and we just thought that it was because we were twins. It wasn't until we were in high school where we realized that we must have something different for people to just come up to us and share their life stories and cry their little eyes out. It never got irritating to us or bothered us to any extent. We just did, said, and talked to whom we were led to do so. In high school I met one of my closest and dearest friends, Pastor John Rials where he started to speak into my life saying that I've been called by G-d to be a prophet. All I have to say is that . . . I ran from it . . .

When we graduated high school we went to Southeast Missouri State University. This is where I ran myself straight into process of submission. In my process of running for the calling on my life I met so many people who would love me in spite of what I would door say to them. I decided to join one of the organizations on campus to set myself apart from my sister and this is when I had my "Jonah Experience". Things got bad and I was swallowed by a situation and it literally almost killed me. I saw myself lying on the floor at least 2 times and each time the Lord said "I have work for you to do . . . Choose Ye this day Whom you will serve." I was pulled out of school broken to pieces, angry, hurt and depressed.

I started to go to a local church in St. Louis and it was good starting out until I started to hit a glass ceiling and I started to see, feel, hear and even smell things again. So my questions started again. This time I felt an urgency in my spirit and no one had time to listen to my questions. As the frustration started to hit its peak I decided I needed to take a break from church so I could see if it was me getting mad for no reason. I kept expressing my frustrations to my sister, Dana, John and Brandon, my brother. A little while after that I finally had it . . . I decided church wasn't for me.

Brandon told me about Agape Time Ministries—City of Refuge and how they were having a Summit and the prophetic was the topic that night. I decided to go and when I stepped in I felt the love consume me. A lot of my expectations I had left so I could be open to what the Lord was going to do that night. I saw at least 10 people I already knew and went to school with. So I immediately felt comfortable. I couldn't believe that there was a place where explanations were freely given if you asked (in your heart and verbally) . . . So I got scared and stayed away for approximately 4 or 5 months. When I decided to go back to see if it was real . . . I was amazed that the Pastors remembered me and hugged me as if they have been waiting on me. I didn't join right then and there . . . but I had an one-on-one with them and expressed my concerns with me, my gifts and callings and they basically said that we can give you some of those answers in G-dly timing but we can teach you how to get the answers yourself by really listening to the Holy Spirit.

Now approximately 10 months later . . . there is a major difference between the young lady in December of 2010 and now (October 2011). I have been taught—through mentorship and fellowship—how to just let go of all the things and people who has hurt me intentionally and unintentionally, the difference between gifts and callings. Most of all I've learned how to hear the voice of the Holy Spirit so that I can get the answers I've had since I was 7 years old of the things I've seen, hear, felt and even smelled.

In the midst of all of that the Lord has dusted off the vision of a ministry He has given me 2 years ago in June 2009. I put dirt on it by making all of the excuses of not being

qualified, running from it, denying it, hiding it, etc. The ministry has been proclaimed to be Selah Music Network it is for the singers, musicians and praise dancers of the St. Louis area. I have been receiving detailed instructions for different events and services that are geared to the singers, musicians and praise dancers since I've gotten the assignment. On October 8th, 2011 it was finally released under the umbrella of ATMI where I got the blessing of Pastor John and Pam Dillon and most of all my brothers and sisters of the house as well.

I am humbled that G-d has chosen me to carry out this assignment but with Pastor John and Pastor Pam as my spiritual parents and my growing family at ATMI who are willing to support, holding me up and most of all praying for me—I know I have no choice but to please the Father as each and every assignment is completed coming from Selah Music Network.

AGAPE ENCOUNTERS

Monday Night Prayer School

Kathy McClenton 1st Leader to be Licensed after 3 yr training

Team on Out Assignment to Overseers Church Pastor Michael E. Johnson—The Refreshing Ministry Oklahoma City, Oklahoma

Team Pictures

Tyrone Nolan Gatekeeper—Prayer—Founder of Warriors Path—2011

Booth, G. W. (1985). *George sweetings great quotes & illustrations.* (p. 107). Dallas, Tex Word.

Chambers, O. (1992). *Edythe draper's book of quotations for Christian world.* (p. 181). Wheaton, III: Wheaton, III Tyndal.

Levy, D. (1993). *The Tabernacle Shadows of the Messiah.* The Friends of Israel Gospel Ministry, Inc.

Maxwell, J. (2006). *21 Irrefutable laws of leadership.*

Mohler, A., Heyford, J., Umidi, J., McMonagle, J. M. D., Humpal, D., &, (1998). *Southern Baptist theological seminary.*

Nance, T. (2002). *God's Armorbearer–How to serve God's leaders.*

New King James Version Bible.

Rabbi Fuer, A. C., Rabbi Scherman, N., & Rabbi Zlotowitz, M. (1985-2004). *Tehillim the book of psalms.* Brooklyn, New York: Me'sorah Publications, Ltd.

Rabbi Kaplan, A., & Sutton, A. (1990). *Innerspace.* Moznaim Publishing Corporation.

Rabbi Scherman, N. (2002) *The prophets. I-II* Samuel (The Rubin Edition ed.). Brooklyn, New York: Me'sorah Publications, Ltd.

Stern, D. (1998). *Complete Jewish Bible.* Clarksville, Maryland: Jewish New Testment Publications, Inc.

Pamela is foremost a woman after God's heart. She has been in ministry for over 25 years and a sought after conference speaker. As the founder of Agape Time Ministries Inc. and co-founder of City of Refuge, she and her husband John are the innovative and apostolic pastors of the unique leadership training facility in St. Louis, Missouri, which equips leaders of all genres in their gifting and callings. Their vision of "Producing and Promoting healthy leaders through mentorship and fellowship has birthed out the most powerful and unique leaders from Arkansas to Jamaica.

In addition Pamela is visionary for the **"Stir up the Gift Summit, Intimate Evening with the Father** and the **"Daughters Retreat"**. The founder of **Prophetic Expressers Dance, Banner, and Mime Team.** Coined the name of Wind-Carriers for the ATMI children's ministry, along with Kristy Snelson. Her list of Godly accomplishments is many. She is a published author of 3 majors equipping books, **"Give the Ashes," The Greater Yes-Answering the Call of God and,"** Thank **God for Pookie'nem"**. Along with numerous word tapes, Pamela has a background in radio and has been hosted on Christian television.

Pamela is a prophetess called by God who understands her purpose in the earth to usher in the glory of God through prayer, sound and movement. Her unique personality and witty sense of humor cause her to be a joy to encounter. She is mother to 4 adult children and 10 grandchildren.